I0087625

LETTERS TO HELENE FROM VIETNAM:

AN OUTLINE OF MY DESCENT INTO PTSD

GUS KAPPLER, MD

Gus Kappler

For more information, email guskappler@yahoo.com

ISBN: 978-0-578-46917-1

Background on the Front Cover Photo

A Bell UH-1 Iroquois helicopter is descending to land. The red cross on a white background indicates that it is a Dust Off Huey.

Below is an aerial view of the 85th Evacuation Hospital in Phu Bai, Vietnam. I took both photographs.

This medivac helicopter was piloted by a twenty- year-old **Warrant Officer, Bob Nevins.**

He and other Dust Off pilots faced imminent death with each flight into Vietnam's enemy infested jungle.

It turns out that Bob flew the wounded to me at the 85th Evac. for the entire year I served. We never crossed paths.

Ten years ago, we met in Albany, NY. He lives near Saratoga Springs, NY, less than an hour away. The war has drawn us close.

Bob is committed to dissolving away the cloud of PTSD for those in all walks of life.

Visit Alliance180.org to meet Bob and learn about his success.

Gus Kappler

Bob Nevins seated in his Dust Off Huey and at Alliance180

Forward
A Vietnam Veteran's Thoughts
After Reading
Letters to Helene

Terence Smith and I bonded at a Homeward Bound Adirondacks Retreat a few winters ago. My responsibility was to facilitate (to get veterans talking) at the evening campfire. Terence was still attempting to understand and deal with his remaining Vietnam demons.

Terence: *"I had no idea that the man who returned from Vietnam was no longer the same person who deployed. "*

My words from the book's *Introduction*: "The man who returned home was different—scarred, angry, and broken. When drinking, he became someone else—someone scarcely recognizable as Gus."

Terence: "The living conditions were awful. Same clothes and no shower for a month, and no bathrooms. Make a shelter every night out of 2 poncho liners, called a hootch. We found sticks for structure and tied them together. Three men to a position set up in a circle. That's if you were not on OP advance warning outside of the circle or on ambush where you were up for the night.

Terence: It was constant danger and constant fear; *after a while you just did not care anymore."*

In the Chapter 17 October 1970 Retrospection, I state that to nullify the constant fear, the grunts accepted that they were going to die.

Terence: *"The mail was the lifeline to the grunt soldiers. It was the only connection we had with the world. Getting a letter or package from home was a big deal. Mail call was something we looked forward to."*

Gus Kappler

v

My 17 October 1970 letter agrees that *the mail was a lifeline*.

Terence:"*The army's position is that the troops were expendable.*" This thought is reiterated by me in Chapter: *Different Pathways*. "Without exception, from Vietnam to the Post 911 wars and conflicts, the active warrior is *abruptly discharged or reassigned into a 'sink or swim' environment.*"

Terence: "When asked what it was like to lose a friend in combat. It was like losing $5.00, it hurt a little, but you get over it quickly."

"New guys showed up from NY, *I don't want to get to know him. It hurts so bad when they take these newbies out of here in pieces.*"

"I think the guy's name was Hawkins from upstate NY. We were friends and in the same squad. In the A Shau Valley we did an air assault to a mountain, then climbed to the top. It was a tough climb to the top. It was hot, rocky and the gear was heavy. Once we got to the top a helicopter brought in a water tank. We drank all our water. It was his turn to fill the canteens that we both carried. He refused because he was tired. It was his turn to fill it because I had done it the last few times. I grabbed his and my water belt and went to the water tank that they had just flown in. An enemy motor round came in; I ducked behind the water tank. So, I waited a few minutes for everything to calm down and filled up the canteens. I walked back to my gear and the medics were on top of Hawkins. *He was hit by shrapnel and medivaced out. He lost his leg.*

That was supposed to be me, and it would have been if he was not so lazy. To this day I just grab what needs to be done and just do it.

Terence Smith, SGT E5, 1st Cavalry Division (Airmobile), Company A, 2nd Battalion, 8th Cavalry, Vietnam, '67-'68. Recipient of The Air Medal.

This eMail Is Better Than Any Medal

Hello,

My name is **Susan Wightman** . My brother, **Craig Owens** , died in December 2023. He was 74 and served in Vietnam when he was 18. Since his death, I have worked hard to get all of his medical records and history, sending many requests to different government agencies. This took about a year but I finally received them by certified mail on a CD - all 1790 pages of them.

I was very young (about 5 years old) when he was drafted. Reading through the records, I saw your name many times. I googled your name to see if I could get some info on you and I found your web page. I ordered your book, "Welcome Home From Vietnam, Finally". It gave me some really good insight into what it was like when he was injured. I appreciated your straightforward descriptions about your experiences.

He was shot during friendly fire by a M16 while sleeping. He was injured on 10/16/1970 near Firebase Tomahawk and taken to the 85th Evac. He then went to Valley Forge on or around 11/25/1970. His injuries were pretty severe and he suffered from circulation issues his entire life but was able to do most things he wanted to do and lived a full and happy life. I'm sure this was because of the great work that you and many other physicians did in Vietnam.

I'm not sure why I'm writing this email but just wanted to let you know that I am very glad that you were there to help my brother when he needed it most. My sister told me that he talked about a physician that took care of him and how he held you in high regard - you made an impact on him even in his condition.

Thanks for taking care of him...

Sue

"Friendly fire," addressed in Letters, refers to being wounded by Americans.

A Few Comments

"The detail that you provide, and the honesty of your writing is truly overwhelming. This should be required reading for anyone trying to understand this period in US history. Congratulations on a job well done!"

Ronald Geiger, MD, Orthopedic Surgeon (Retired)
Massachusetts General Hospital, Boston, MA

"The concept of the letters and then the digital version of the letters works well.

I loved the Retrospective pages. I believe those remarks add credibility to the content of the letters. My favorite parts here and in "Welcome Home" were the links you added within the content to add integrity to "Welcome Home" stories and add a resource for the readers to research and find more answers.

Congratulations, my friend, on yet another way to reach our Veterans who may be suicidal, and thank you on my behalf for taking a stance on the sink or swim philosophy"

Bill Sheehan, Author of *Together We Served."* Bill served as a Navy Corpsman treating wounded Marines in Vietnam

Dedication

I dedicate *Letters* to my little sister, **Helene**

Parry, who saved the fourteen letters

I wrote to her from Vietnam.
That correspondence is the essence of this book.

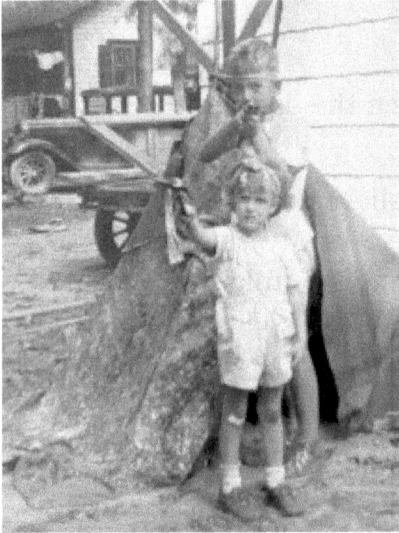

She has always stood by me.

It began behind our garage in Lake Ronkonkoma, LI, NY when playing as members of the Nissaquogies tribe.

Introduction

Over half a century ago, shortly after returning home from my tour in Vietnam, I uttered in a drunken stupor a phrase that haunts me to this day: "Kill all the fucking Vietnamese."

Did that reprehensible statement truly come from me? Once home, my PTSD had surfaced, and I was lost in a fog of anger and pain. I had no idea that the man who returned from Vietnam was no longer the same person who had deployed. The Gus who went to war was a surgeon, trained to honor and preserve life. That person only wanted to be the best doctor he could be. He was compassionate, dedicated, and hopeful.

My service in Vietnam as an Army trauma surgeon at the 85th Evacuation Hospital exposed me daily to the devastating effects of war-mutilated bodies, shattered minds, broken souls, and warrior suicides. Witnessing such horrors changed me, but I was unaware of how deeply.

My transformation was insidious. My brain, protecting me from the unbearable sights and sounds, employed mechanisms that I only now understand. I was unconscious of how I was slipping into a darkness of rage and the dependence on alcohol to find some semblance of comfort amid my chaos.

The man who returned home was different-scarred, angry, and broken. When drinking, he became someone else—someone scarcely recognizable as Gus.

Recently, when my sister, **Helene,** unearthed a box of fourteen letters I had written to her from Vietnam. Letter by letter the black-and-white pages documented my war zone downward spiral, from hope and purpose to anger and despair - PTSD.

That descent reached a crescendo at my roommate's goodbye party, when anesthetic from alcohol, I jumped off a bunker and suffered a fracture-dislocation of my right elbow. This accident was potentially career ending.

My wife **Robin** , my anchor, often asked, "How did you become so angry? When did you start relying on alcohol to find peace?" Her questions, though painful, were a mirror into my hidden suffering.

Through many years of research, I've come to understand that PTSD may result in anyone exposed to traumatic events. No one is immune. It does not discriminate based on strength, character, or background. It's a natural reaction to extraordinary circumstances.

Thanks to Helene, **you and I** may follow my distortion and identify the traumas causing my pain. But my story doesn't end there. Once I returned home and confronted the contamination of my soul, I sought ways to resurrect the Gus I once was - gentle, hopeful, dedicated to life. Still, I would continue to live with persistent anger.

Hear Gus's anger at *Echoes of the Vietnam War* on this link: *A Vietnam Veterans Memorial Fund Podcast: Gus Is Still Angry:* *https://echoes-of-the-vietnam-war.simplecast.com/episodes/gus-kappler*

In my **Epilogue** we will discover that PTSD is not only a predictable consequence of exposure to devastating events but also a challenge that may be managed and overcome.

1

With time, I accomplished my restoration. Healing is possible with the adjustments I instituted. Even in our darkest moments, there is hope.

A most salient question is " *Can PTSD be prevented?* " I will also discuss that approach.

Principal South Vietnam Landmarks

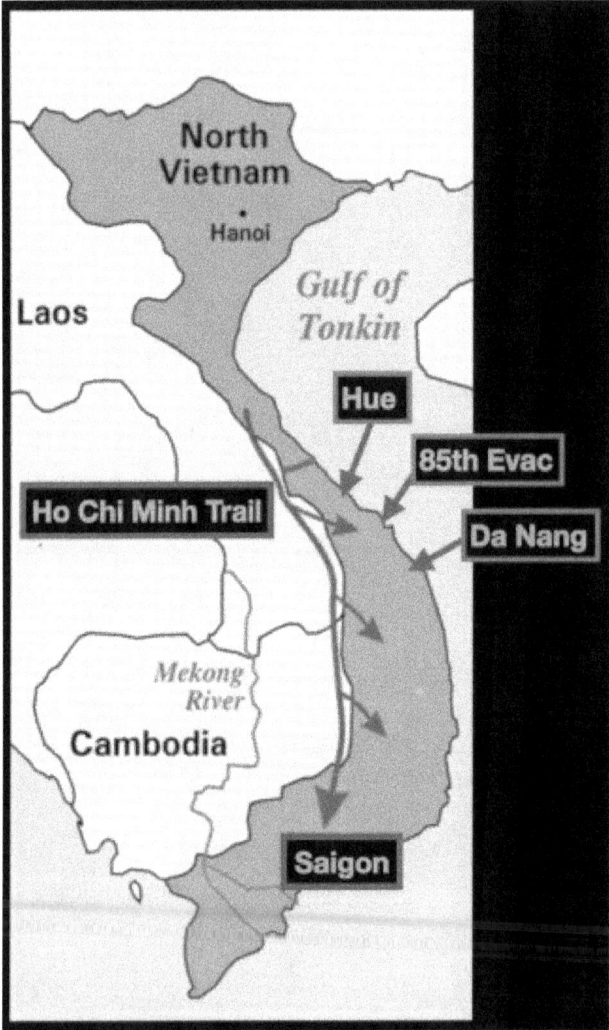

Table of Contents

Prologue

I'm a PTSD survivor. At age thirty I succumbed to the disorder when serving in a combat zone.

Ed Tick, PhD in *War and the Soul* considers trauma to be the "rape of one's soul."

I now understand the evolution, over a year's interval, of a sheltered, naive, middle class young adult American into an angry, detached, disillusioned, and excessively drinking veteran.

I did not consider myself changed when returning to the United States, but in reality, I was no longer the Gus that flew from Dallas to begin my Vietnam adventure. The inevitable ***war zone change*** had occurred.

Some of that change has persisted. As other veterans, I reflect on Vietnam daily - especially when a helicopter flies overhead. At the 85th Evacuation Hospital, not a minute went by without that sound above us.

Here are similar responses from my Facebook correspondence:

David Harbour: "Is it ever going to be over?" **James Cook:** "I'm there more than I'm here." **George Dale:** "We never left."

Ed Letourneau: "The truth is, no one who was part of the war ever comes completely home. War only ends for the dead."

7

As Janina Fisher, PhD, relates "Traumatic experiences leave a *living legacy* of effects that often persist for years and decades after the event is over."

I have successfully reintegrated into a peaceful society. I enjoyed a successful solo surgical practice and retired in 2000. However, I continue to be very angry about the needless and pointless sacrifice all Vietnam warriors made, especially those afflicted by Agent Orange, maimed, and KIA. To my embarrassment that anger at times will erupt inappropriately.

For you, your family, and friends to address the life altering challenge of PTSD, the factors predisposing you to this disorder must be understood.

Let me help you by analyzing the fourteen letters from Vietnam my sister, Helene, saved.

The military, nurses, police, EMT's, doctors, lawyers, first responders, couple's violence suffers, those in midlife crisis, and any individual whose life is exposed to excessive mental stress will benefit from the book's discussion.

Helene's fourteen letters from Vietnam are of varying lengths. I have been reminded that my handwriting was and is atrocious.

Therefore, three sections appear in each chapter.

a) The first page of the original letter.

b) The entire letter printed in a readable font.

c) A retrospective of my personal Vietnam experiences that prompted the words I wrote. I will at times expand on background information that helped shape those words. More timely thoughts were also inserted.

My *Epilogue* will expand on issues that I consider relative to my story and present a roadmap for healing.

I apologize to readers offended by a few areas of raw or demeaning language and expletives in my letters.

But that was me in Vietnam.

"LEAVING ON A JET PLANE"

"As I was preparing to leave for the Dallas Airport my wife Robin was softly weeping, flooding reddened eyes with tears. She appeared pitiful. My strong wife's demeanor now conveyed panic, my desertion, loss, fear, and disbelief. She expressed without words "How could you do this to me?""

I had no choice. The US Army had ordered me for a year to Vietnam as a trauma surgeon.

The emotion of that moment was overwhelming. We knew this day would come but the devastation of actually separating was extremely heart wrenching. I frequently relive that moment."

Excerpted from *Welcome Home From Vietnam, Finally, A Vietnam Trauma Surgeon's Memoir*

12 September 1970

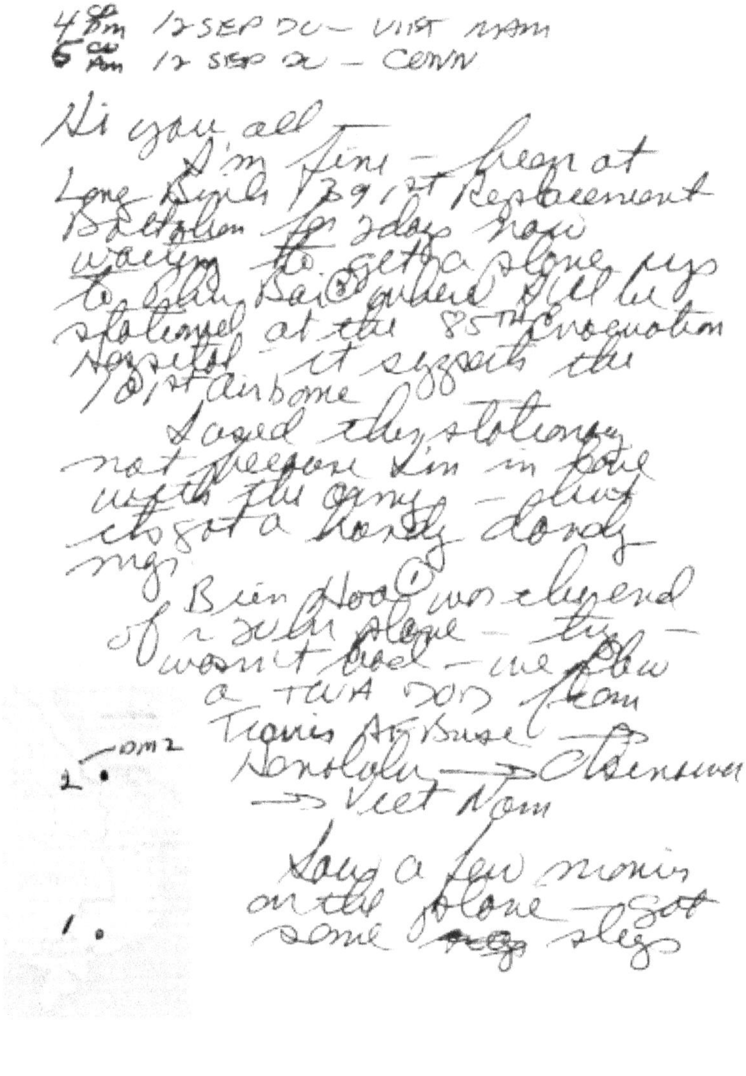

4 PM 12 SEP 70 – VIET NAM
5 AM 12 SEP 70 – CONN

Hi you all –
I'm fine – been at
Long Binh 90th Replacement
Battalion for 2 days now
waiting to get a plane up
to Phu Bai where I'll be
stationed at the 85th evacuation
Hospital. It supports the
101st Airborne.
Saved the stationery –
not because I'm in love
with the army – plus
it's got a handy dandy
map.
Bien Hoa was the end
of a 20 hr plane trip –
wasn't bad – we flew
a TWA 707 from
Travis Air Base →
Honolulu → Okinawa
→ Viet Nam
Saw a few movies
on the plane – got
some sleep

DMZ
2.
1.

Complete Letter

4pm 12 Sept 70 - Vietnam

6:00 12 Sept 70 - Conn Hi

you all -

I'm fine - Been at the Long Binh 391 st Replacement Battalion for 2 days now waiting to get a plane up to Phu Bai (#2) where I'll be stationed at the 85th Evacuation Hospital - it supports the 101st Airborne.

I used this stationary not because I'm in love with the Army - but it's got a handy dandy map .

Bein Hoa (#1) was the end of a 20 hour plane trip - wasn't bad - we flew a TWA 707 from Travis Air Force Base to Honolulu to Okinawa to Vietnam - saw a few movies on the plane and got some sleep

and met a lot of guys - This country is peaceful from the sky - even pretty - but the sand bags, barbed wire metal remind one there's a war.

I'm anxious to get to my station - this waiting around is bad news - I even finished the Godfather - a good book - I think I'm going to have to check out Robin's dad.

Well I'll keep in touch - I'll write more once I get settled -

Love
Eddie

Retrospective

My 12 September letter to my younger sister, **Helene**, reflects that of a tourist having flown to a distant land for a vacation.

On the TWA bare bones flight, I looked military in my khaki summer uniform with a caduceus on my right lapel and a gold major's leaf on the left. I was the oldest passenger. Both me and the teenage soldiers surrounding me had no idea of what was waiting for us in Vietnam's jungles. But they were optimistic about their futures.

At Long Binh, during my first overnight in Vietnam, I bunked with another Major who was going "back to the world," home. Small arms fire erupted about 2 am. I stood up to see what was going on. The veteran Major was on the floor - my first lesson that the enemy was there to kill Americans.

I did reference sandbags and barbed wire. This barrier was actually called concertina wire that was covered with multiple small-pointed razors.

The comment about Robin's dad related to his being Sicilian.

I could not wait to get back in the operating room, my sanctuary. That said, I had never encountered war wounds and the mutilation accompanying them.

In retrospect I know I was headed for a rude awakening. That is the story of *Letters To Helene From Vietnam.*

In my 12 September 1970 letter I did not relate my emotional separation from Robin. The defense mechanism, *compartmentalization* , had begun. My brain was hijacking emotionally traumatic experiences and hiding them from my conscious mind to avoid mental discomfort or anxiety.

However, with time these traumas could and would be exposed. The subtle process of developing PTSD had begun.

AMERICAN PSYCHOLOGICAL ASSOCIATION

Compartmentalization

Updated on 04/19/2018

n. a **defense mechanism** in which *thoughts and feelings that seem to conflict or to be incompatible are isolated from each other in separate and apparently impermeable psychic compartments.*

From now on let's substitute the word **Bury** for the tongue twister **Compartmentalization.**

24 SEPTEMBER 1970

24 SEP — PHU BAI   THURS — 3⁰⁰pm

24 SEP — ROCKVILLE   THURS — 2 AM

Hi Helene + Jim
      Helen ann + Jamie —

    Got your letter today — it took 5 day air mail — not bad at all. Phu Bai is pronounced Foo BY. As you may know by now it's physically about the worst place in Viet Nam - dust, mud, plywood hooches to live in — you have to steal, trade, bargain etc to obtain a few items to make living comfortable — but the people here are great — food well does and very well trained Marys Brd + Rolin — Rogecher should have 4 Rolls of film showing this place, this hospital (it to be a series of plywood palaces), my trip to Saigon + to Hue.

This Complete Letter is long therefore, it is segmented with individual Retrospections

24 Sept - Rockville - Thurs 2:00 pm

Hi Helene + Jim

Helene Ann + Jamie

-

Got your letter today, - it took 5 day air mail - not bad at all.

Phu Bai is pronounced FOO BY. As you may know by now it's physically about the worst place in Vietnam - dust, mud, plywood hooches to live in

 - you have to steal, trade, bargain etc to obtain a few items to make living comfortable

- but the people here are great - hard workers and very well trained.

Mom, Dad, and Robin - together should have 4 rolls of film showing this place, the hospital (it too is a series of plywood shacks), my trip to Saigon + Hue.

The monsoon season up here begins in mid October and lasts ~ 4 months

Retrospection

The 24 September letter to Helene is my first since arriving at the 85th Evacuation Hospital in Phu Bai. It's newsy and reflects our daily experiences.

"Phu Bai's all right" was known countrywide as our mocking motto for that place was the "armpit" of Vietnam.

The "5 finger discount" worked well in supplying one's needs. Stealing became acceptable in wartime.

Members of the 85th Evacuation Hospital family in Phu Bai, the medics, specialists, support services, nurses, and doctors were committed to caring for soldiers' wounds and illnesses. The wounded received state-side and at times better than state-side care. Advanced techniques in patient care and surgery were explored without fear of litigation.

During the monsoon season the sun rarely appeared. The sky was overcast and the surrounding air entombed us in constant foggy wetness. If it were not raining large droplets, we would be assaulted by a constant heavy mist. Our fatigues and bedding were always damp. This problem was solved by applying an electric blanket to our cot, keeping the bedding and our next day's clothes dry.

A 100-watt light bulb in my metal locker worked well on the hanging clothes. An electric blanket in a combat zone - sounds crazy.

Letter Continues

I operated on a poor guy last week - he was booby trapped - I amputated both his legs above the knee - layered his right arm wide open - resected 4 feet of his small intestine, 2 feet of his large intestine, fixed up a battered urinary bladder and repaired torn major blood vessels in the abdomen -

took 8 hours + 76 pints of blood - That poor bastard!!

He was laying on the x-ray table + asked "What have I done to deserve this?" - I couldn't answer him

- I re-operated on him twice + his kidneys failed - the only place in Vietnam with a dialysis unit is the 3rd Field Hospital in Saigon

- therefore, I Medivaced him in a C-130 to Saigon (you'll see pictures of this). Worked on him a few days then - he died -

I got to tour the city - quite interesting - the people all hate our guts - but hustle the hell out of you to get your money - I took pictures of garbage piled in the streets, Buddhist temples, street cars, buildings, market-place etc.

Again, check with mom and dad + Robin.

Retrospective Continued

"What did I do to deserve this?" were the severely wounded grunt's last coherent words as he lay shivering on the cold hard X-ray table. I had no answer. I would have decompensated if I had not **buried** the boy's desperation.

This patient was on patrol sweeping through an abandoned Viet Cong (VC) campsite. A piece of Styrofoam caught his inquisitive adolescent eye. Just as the enemy knew from years of fighting westerners, both French and American, this eighteen-year-old kid picked up the styrofoam and "blew himself to pieces."

His original surgery was long and tedious. His post-op course required re-operation and additional blood transfusions. His kidneys failed and his condition necessitated kidney dialysis.

I had poured my heart and soul into caring for him. I wished to accompany him into the hospital and was rejected by the staff of the 3rd Field Hospital in Saigon. I mentally closed that patient's chapter and decided to casually tour Saigon - It was *buried.*

"...the people all hate our guts..." So, why the hell were

we there? Their hatred was easy to understand.
The United States-

1) invaded their sovereign country.

2) changed its leadership to President Diem and then assassinated him when it did not work out.

19

3) covered up the fact that we were not winning the war until the Tet Offensive in '68-'69 exposed our folly.

4) attempted to "win hearts and minds" by wantonly killing fathers, mothers, women, young men, and children

5) burning their rice crops and villages.

The lesson not learned was that America's powerful military machine failed to best an indigenous army whose advantage was knowing their "backyard." They, more importantly, could retreat into a massive tunneling network for protection, sustenance, medical care, and rearming.

To the lethal detriment of our troops, the Pentagon leadership never thought it important to learn their enemy's history and culture.

Look at the outcomes for Russia and America in Afghanistan.

Please read *Dereliction of Duty* by H. R. McMaster and *The Afghan Papers* by Craig Whitlock. Both books tell the same sickening story of egos, legacies, and the wish for recognition and advancement either militarily or politically perpetuating mindless wars.

Letter Continues

We have a football team - like MASH -

We'll fly to Da Nang Sunday + play the 95th Evac Hospital- drink some beer + come back. Yesterday

I flew - in a helicopter to Hue (WAY) - what a beautiful trip - took 10 minutes. We each go (that is the surgeons) one day a week to the ARVN (Vietnamese Army) Hospital and help their surgeons operate, teach them and make rounds with them. It was quite an experience- the patients are Viet Cong as well as ARVN. The place is 40 years behind the US in knowledge - very superstitious - but we can teach them a lot - this is a MEDCAP program - you'll see pictures of this too.

My time has been pretty well occupied with operating, trips etc- you look for things to do to fill up your day over here - I can see the limits of my compound ~ 100 meters on in any direction around me. So it's just like being in jail

This is my 17th day in country - I'm the FNG - Fucking new guy - can't wait till someone new comes so I can get rid of that title.

We have a movie every nite at 9:00 pm at the club - another shack - but with a fan + booze. There are a few other clubs at other compounds nearby - I'll probably get to them.

As you may know - a guy by the name of Roger King is here with me - I was a year behind him during the residency.

Well you all be good - Love
Eddie

Retrospective Continued

Our 85th Evac flag football team was undefeated versus other hospitals. It may have helped that our quarterback was **Leo Flynn**, MD, an orthopedic surgeon, who had been the back-up QB for Auburn University. *Leo died of Agent Orange related heart disease in his mid-fifties. One of eight from our seventeen medical staff who were affected by the Agent Orange travesty to die.*

Really happy stuff!

The 85th Evac's contribution to "winning hearts and minds" was our MEDCAP trips to Hue and the ARVN hospital. On my first trip as a naive newbie, I inquired of regular Army Captain **Fred Brockschmidt,** RN, a world class nurse anesthetist, why he had a M16. He responded, "we are at war." *Fred also died a few years ago from an Agent Orange derived cancer.*

We would bring to Hue our outdated blood that could not be transfused into our wounded. We also brought our expertise in anesthesia and surgery that was usually waisted. We stopped going because the risk of getting killed outweighed any good we could have accomplished.

The Vietnamese Army Hospital lacked the funds to fully support any aspect of health care delivery. There were little if any anesthetic agents, gowns, gloves, drapes, and instruments. Most wounded soldiers were admitted and observed.

All the Vietnamese physicians were only partially trained. Their expertise barely matched that of our Army medics. They resorted to growing and selling vegetables, chickens and their eggs, and rabbits to buy supplies.

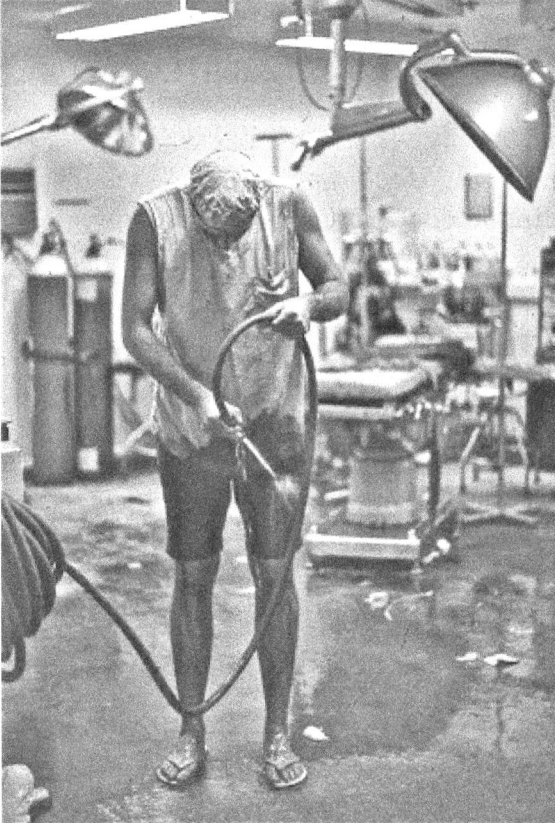

Gus hosing off the blood bath

Our existence was periods of boredom alternating with the organized chaos of reviving and operating on multiple wounded. When finished we were covered in sticky metallic smelling blood from the waist down. The mess would fill our combat boots. The Vietnamese mamma sons who cleaned for us complained. Wearing Bermuda shorts and flip- flops solved that problem.

After surgery we partied, i.e. drinking excessively and sleeping as long as possible. In retrospect, I now realize we were *self-medicating* to numb any compartmentalized trauma that may have escaped its confinement in our subconscious .

That issue never entered our minds. The alcohol certainly helped to
bury our psychic trauma. Our PTSD was growing invasive roots.

The first face at the 85th I encountered was that of **Roger King.** What a miracle! He advised me that everything would be alright. And eventually, he was right.

Roger and I both trained at the Medical College of Virginia in Richmond. I chose that program because it was chaired by David Hume, MD, a young aggressive clinical and research surgeon who was active in the early days of kidney transplant surgery. We got to operate on day one.

When I was there, he and the MCV neurologists were the first in the country to redefine death as being "brain dead." The transplant surgeons did not have to wait for the heart to stop. That way the neurologically dead patient's functioning heart and lungs would continue to keep the kidneys viable while waiting to be transplanted.

For a critical slant to the new definition, read *The Organ Thieves* : https://www.nytimes.com/2020/08/18/books/review/the-organ- thieves-chip-jones.html

We were at times overwhelmed with Richmond's trauma and given early responsibility for decision making. Roger completed his surgical training a year prior to me but was sent to Vietnam during the second year of active duty. Our time at the 85th Evac. overlapped by six months. Roger and I became the go-to surgeons. The ED and OR staff marveled at our ability to anticipate each other's moves to accomplish life-saving surgery.

Roger died last year from an aggressive prostatic cancer derived from Agent Orange exposure.

That's the third Agent Orange death of my 85th Evac. colleagues I'm reminded of in the first two letters from Vietnam to my sister, Helene.

We were totally unaware that Agent Orange was being sprayed. Therefore, we were unaware of the extreme toxicity of Agent Orange's predictable containment - Dioxin. We never conceived that hundreds of thousands of Americans would derive major illnesses from this herbicide. In the US and Vietnam, hundreds of thousands have died from Agent Orange derived diseases.

I said goodbye to my wife and children, to be gone for a year. I abruptly flew to Vietnam and the unknown. Then there was the hot, sweaty, foul-smelling travel up-country to Phu Bai and the 85th Evacuation Hospital, halfway between Hue and Da Nang. All these experiences were mentally devastating. Yet, to my eventual detriment, my mind could **bury** them.

During my service at the 85th Evac, our hospital treated 50% of the American wounded in Vietnam. We were at the first exit of the Ho Chi Minh Trail, not more than 40 kilometers from Laos (look back to Principal Vietnam Landmarks). If the wounded made it to the 85th Evac. alive, they had a 96% chance of survival.

All of us at the 85th witnessed the ugly devastation of war on body, mind, and soul. We dealt with the horrors of war daily. We grew very close and shared a genuine love (brotherhood).

Roger and I were a unique entity. I have never experienced a professional relationship as intense and successful.

Roger King, we at the 85th Evac will miss you, especially me.

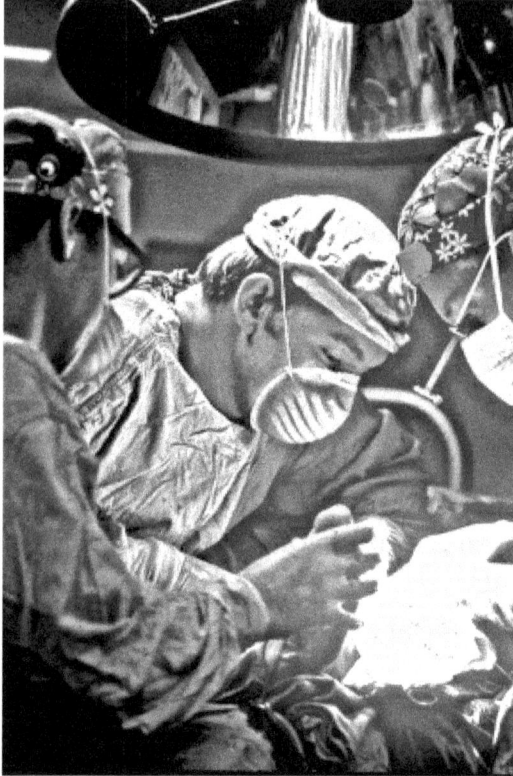

Medtech "Tree" Dave Anderson, Gus, and Roger King at the 85th Evac. "Tree" died of Agent Orange triggered colon cancer.

17 October 1970

17 October 70 - Sat - 4:00pm Hi

there -

Thank you for all those letters - I've got the Parry household routine down pat for now -

Things are going along fine - I've been busy patching up the poor son - of - bitches who get shot up by the Viet Cong, accidents, attempted murder by their men, and "friendly" fire - ie GI's shooting other GI's by mistake -

This place is a damn waste!

It's funny - I heard stories of 2nd Lieutenants and Sergeants bring shot in the back in combat - here if you don't like your commander you throw a fragmentation grenade into his hootch - BANG - Blood, guts, brains splatter all over the place - a real nice place - Vietnam and these bastards aren't worth fighting for - they'd sell us out + do to the highest bidder.

Enough of that stuff - but this place is an eye opener -

Other than operating, my major concerns were fixing up my hooch, photographing the various aspects of the 85th compound, and shopping in area PX's (Phu Bai and Da Nang) and utilizing PACEX in Japan. We also ordered items from Penny's and Sears catalogues.

I finished my hooch - looks great - Robin will have pictures of it. - the OR, ER etc.

I got my new Minolta camera - taking pictures in the OR without a flash -

Gus Kappler

I ordered your Christmas gift thru PACEX a few days ago - hope it gets there on time - I'm going crazy ordering things. Jim if you want a camera or anything - the prices are ~ 1/3 - 1/2 of state side prices + you'll only have to pay duty on the amount over $50 - since it's classified as a gift _ if you talk to the local post office maybe you can get them to overlook the duty (it has been done) - Robin has a catalog - for cameras it's 17% (duty) - so for example a Minolta SRT 101 is $131 - Duty on $80 is ~ $13.50 - State side the camera cash ~ $325 at least.

Tonite is a Hi BY party. The people DEROSING - (means going home) and the new guys (me and others) are given a party once a month.

We're going to have a Halloween party + then stay DRUNK from Thanksgiving until Christmas holidays are over - might sober up by new years -

Well take care - I'm doing fine - got a nice place to live, now adjusted to the place, have a booze stock that doesn't quit - have ordered a Stereo Cassette recorder to sex this place up

Love Eddie

Retrospective

Receiving letters from home maintained our connection to sanity and comforting conversation. *Vietnam was truly an out of world experience.*

The casualties were from enemy fire, vehicle and workplace accidents, disputes among soldiers (everyone was armed), attempted suicide, friendly fire, and attempted murder of leaders in the field that were too aggressive in pursuing the enemy.

Viet Cong booby traps were most of the cases. The VC were resourceful in utilizing our unexploded ordnance - grenades, artillery shells, land mines, bullets, and bombs. The jungle was close to impenetrable and American patrols gravitated to walking established trails. A big mistake, for the VC were masters at disguising the mutilating weapon's placement.

Following the explosion, white hot fragments, traveling at 2500 feet per second and impacting with 6000 horsepower of kinetic energy, inflicted unimaginable destruction of arms, legs, torso, and genitalia. The human body is essentially the density of water and the shock wave resulting from dispersal of the kinetic energy, the *Ballistic Shock Wave,* devitalized additional tissue that required debridement.

Walking patrol was tantamount to playing Russian Roulette in not knowing if, when, and where the booby trap would be tripped. Does one bury this challenge or just accept the risk? Many grunts dealt by assuming they would be killed, and no precautions could protect them. They just fought with abandon.

There were two major chapters to the Vietnam War - before and after Tet '68-'69. Before Tet the *fabric of the Army* was intact. The chain of command was respected and the soldiers fought with purpose having been led to believe their bloody sacrifices were effectively winning the war and protecting democracy.

The Tet Offensive conducted by the Viet Cong (VC) and the North Vietnamese Army (NVA) resulted from the unrecognized (by the Americans) infiltration of enemy forces into major cities up and down South Vietnam. All their firepower was unleashed at the same time. Cites were lost to the enemy. The battle to regain the US Embassy in Saigon and the bloody urban fighting in Hue are well documented. In the end, all the enemy gains were repulsed.

The embarrassing outcome of Tet '68 presented to the world that all the American military and political propaganda was a lie. *We were not winning.*

The Tet Offensive by the VC and NVA was the game changer.

Our country's leaders had decided to end the war. However, the loss would certainly tarnish political and military legacies. The drawdown was gradual, and kids were still being slaughtered without an effort to win.

Norman Camp, M.D wrote in his *US Army Psychiatry in the Vietnam War* that a warrior's unit supplied strength, protection, love, stability, rationalization, a moral base, cohesiveness, and discipline. Before Tet 1968 the *"fabric"* of the Army was strong having been woven securely by healthy units. After Tet 1968, once the warriors learned of our government's deceit, the unit cohesion weakened considerably, and the *fabric of the Army frayed.* PTS, Suicides, psychosis, racial tensions, lack of discipline, fragging, and heroin ('72: 1 in 8) usage escalated.

Discipline eroded.

Dr. Norman Camp served in Da Nang at the same time I was at the 85th Evac.

"Friendly Fire" did not occur often, but it was part of the fog of war

- either by accident or on

purpose. "Fragging" had become

commonplace.

The grunts, average age twenty-two years, realized that they would have to protect themselves. *Who wanted to be the last to die in Vietnam?* The grunts just wanted to go home. Self-preservation and protecting their brothers trumped the threat of becoming KIA.

They took control - "do not risk our lives needlessly." First and Second Lieutenants and senior EM's (Enlisted Men) learned to "lighten up ti-ti (a little)." If either was too risk prone on patrol a warning non- lethal smoke grenade would explode near-by. If change did not occur, the fragmentation grenade solved the problem. A M16 round in the back of a gung-ho leader was not lost on others in charge.

"...these bastards aren't worth fighting for...." was a common tenant in general and on our 85th compound. We all were fearful of trusting the Vietnamese. The interpreter in the ED that befriended us was found to be VC. *He was disappeared.* The Vietnamese workers stole everything that was not nailed down - food, tools, diesel fuel, utensils, et.al.

"This place is a damn waste!" - universally agreed to by most Americans in Vietnam. The Vietnamese on both sides hated us, we were certainly not winning "hearts and minds" when slaughtering them, burning their villages, and destroying their crops. But, our allies in South Vietnam learned how to manipulate the Americans for the benefit of themselves.

With being incarcerated on the 85th Evac. compound and time on our hands we had incentive to beautify our hooches, tape, and party at the "O" Club and in our hooch.

I explored many aspects of photography. I learned about depth of field, of stops, and macro, wide angle, zoom, and telephoto lenses. Even tried to persuade my brother-in-law, Jimmy, to get involved.

Photographically preserving my experiences in Vietnam was paramount in recording history for future generations - especially in the area of battlefield trauma and the surgical techniques utilized to prevent death and maintain functionality of the victim. We repaired all vessels primarily or with a vein graft - at the time of the first surgery.

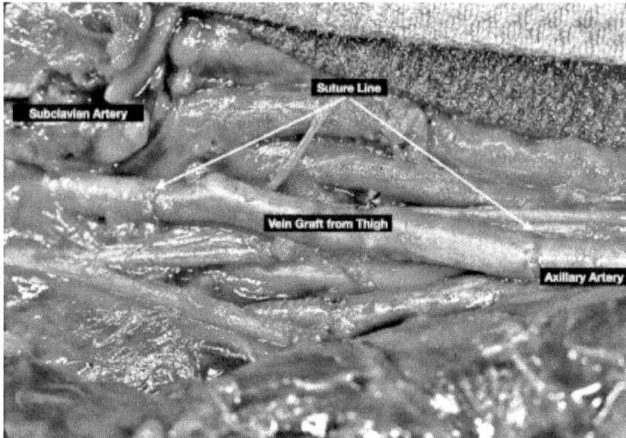

Saphenous (thigh) vein graft from the Subclavian Artery to the Axillary Artery, reconstituting blood flow to the arm and hand.

In WWII the repair of injured blood vessels was discouraged. Major arteries in extremities were ligated and resulted in a twenty-five percent amputation rate. In Korea blood vessel repair was in its infancy. In Vietnam, just about every surgeon could perform this procedure. In the post 911 wars Damage Control Surgery was instituted. Initially a plastic tube was inserted to bridge the gap in the traumatically divided blood vessel to preserve blood flow to the extremity. The arterial repair was delayed - to be performed in a controlled and better equipped environment.

I wore surgical gloves size 71/2. The scrub medic would slip a size 8 over the sterile gloves so I could hold the unsterile camera. The circulating medic would then remove the bigger gloves and sterility was maintained.

Photos were taken of pre and post operative X-rays, injuries before and after surgery, the controlled chaos of the ED and operating room, and our hospital team. Our lives outside the hospital were fully documented.

For color trauma slides please visit **My Vietnam Battlefield Trauma Experience:** https://youtu.be/ywIabgx4zeU

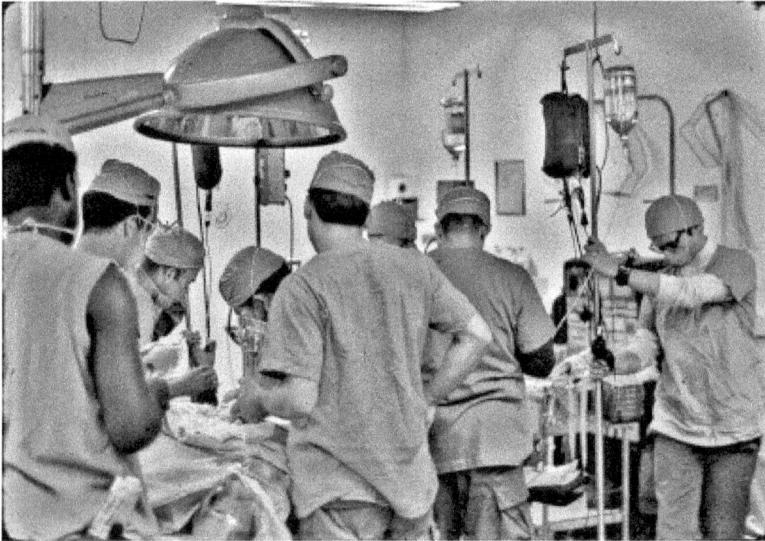

Controlled chaos in an 85th Evac operating room. All hands were on deck.

I've shown my Vietnam trauma, 85th Evac. lifestyle slides, and my PTSD research hundreds of times over the past half century - locally, nationally, and internationally.

The Hi - Bye Parties were bittersweet. *Hi* to the newbies and *By* to the lucky ones going back to the "world" - to DEROS home (Date Estimated Return From Overseas).

The entire compound gathered in a large Army dull green painted plywood shack with a corrugated metal roof. It was elevated on short stilts to avoid flooding during the monsoons. That drab building was our officer's club, but it had a nice bar and was well stocked. We loved it.

Working intimately together caring for the wounded, maimed, and dying developed unbreakable bonds of love. We mourned for ourselves when friends left and felt sorry for newbies. That love is as strong as ever for those of us from the 85th Evac still alive. Our reunions are those of a loving family still looking for answers and redemption.

Why a Vietnam War? Why do our minds return there on a daily? Will we ever be capable of expelling our demons? After fifty-five years the reunions are sought out to "heal."

Again, there is reference to excessive drinking - the self-medicating was becoming more prevalent in assisting in the *burying* and descending into PTSD.

We could order items from Penney's and Sears to spruce up our hooch's interior. I made shelves from the wooden boxes within which mortar rockets were shipped. I could not do much with the yellowed OD green mosquito netting over my cot, but it did prevent being infected with malaria.

24 October 1970

24 OCT 70
SAT - PHU BAI

Hi Helene + Jim

Sorry Cornell lost - but sounds like it was a football game worth seeing. No bowl [illegible] -

We've been busy - past 2 days we've been operating on [illegible] consultation - you know ARVNs (Viet [illegible]) - Some rockets hit the perimeter + 2 guys got frags through their upper abdomen - one bled to death on the table the other got 22 units of blood + had half his intestine, stomach + liver removed.

Then the VC booby trapped a door + a guy's daughter got blown up - she died in the ER - + I took out 3/4 of his liver + he's doing fine -

Complete Letter

24 Oct 70

Sat - Phu Bai

Hi Helene + Jim

Sorry Cornell lost - but sounds like it was a football game worth seeing. No bombs though -

We've been busy - past 2 days we've been operating on GOOK casualties - you know ARVANs (Vietnamese). Some rockets hit the perimeter + 2 gooks got frags through their upper abdomen - one bled to death on the table the other got - 60 units of blood + had half his intestine, stomach + liver removed -

Then the VC booby trapped a door + a gook couple got blown up - she died in the ER - + I took out 2/3rds of his liver + he's doing fine

We've started to liven this place up - had 2 housewarmings this week in my playboy hooch - and still hungover but - I did that case with half a load on - but we both survived it.

Tonite the "Ink Spots" - an old group with new faces - will play here - see if I can't pinch a few bottoms - at the office that is -

Thank you for the cards - they have some here but poor -

We got our refrigerator the other day - The PX sells Coke, 7-Up, Budweiser, Ginger Ale it's by the case so we all stocked up.

My liquor cabinet is also stocked for an "emergency" -

We've had only mild monsoons - today its sunny - usually rains each day - not bad - it should get worse next month - no sweat - got all the booze I need - I get all your letters fine - thanks

Love Eddie

Retrospective

My dad and I went to Cornell. My parents most likely took Helene and Jim to a game at Yale.

Several ARVN (South Vietnamese Army) soldiers were wounded protecting the 85th Evac. perimeter. One bled out. I operated on another, repaired and removed portions of his stomach and intestines. I then resected (removed) the huge right lobe of his liver - a risky, bloody, and challenging operation requiring excessive blood with a dubious outcome. He survived. In the Post 911 wars casualties with bleeding liver injuries were packed (applying pressure with towels) to avoid resection. Most livers stop bleeding with this approach thus, avoiding commitment to actual time consuming and risky surgery.

Not long after my first liver resection I successfully performed the identical surgery on a Vietnamese male whose hooch was booby trapped by the VC for aiding the Americans.

It's amazing how easily I switched from resecting portions of liver to sprucing up my hooch. ***Burying again.***

Usage of the term "Gook" (originating during the Korean War) and "Dink" were associated with dehumanizing the VC and NVA - as were "Jap" and "Nip," (Japanese), "Hun" "Kraut" "Heinie" (Germans) in WWII, and "Towelhead" (Muslims and Arabs), "Hajji" (Iraqi) in our Post 911 Wars.

Enemy humans became "subhuman", and less guilt was associated with killing them. This process, according to Ed Tick, PhD., is an important factor when considering the evolution of the "moral injury" of war (*War and the Soul*).

I did not trust a single Vietnamese I met during my Vietnam service. As previously noted, our ED interpreter turned out to be VC. He was disappeared. I too was caught up in the Vietnam quagmire and used the slur.

I had more respect for an enemy, the NVA (North Vietnamese Army) and Kit Carson Scouts (NVA now on our side) wounded. They were more educated, dedicated, and appreciative.

My degradation of the Vietnamese softened over the years. In 2013 I met **Mytrang Do** at Weill Cornell Medicine (WCM). She was a first- year medical student I facilitated in Problem Based Learning: Human Structure and Function. Emigrating at age thirteen to Louisiana she thrived, did great at LSU, and was now excelling at WCM. We bonded and she healed my wartime wounds. Please watch **Wounds We Feel At Home,** an Albany, NY PBS video: https://video.wmht.org/video/ the-wounds-we-feel-at-home-jhtabp/. It contains the audio of a tape recording I sent to my parents from Vietnam which reflects my state of mind. A segment shows Mia and I interacting in New York - on 69th Street and in the lab.

She and Anfei, also in my WCM class, married, completed their MD-PhD degrees, love their young son, Aaron, and completed their respective residency programs. Mia in Dermatology and Anfei in Ophthalmology. Robin and I attended their wedding near New Orleans and were considered their American grandparents. I must admit that before flying there I was concerned about being surrounded

by Vietnamese and what reservations some may have had. As it turned out we were treated as part of their family.

Mia and Anfei visited us Memorial Day weekend 2025 at our home in Amsterdam, NY. I exposed six-year-old Aaron to the rural experiences of identifying deer tracks, planting an herb garden, and walking with my English Setter bird dog, Codi.

Our personal relationships are as strong as ever.

Anfei, Mia, Aaron, Gus, and Robin

5 November 1970

5 NOV 70   THURS ~ 10 P

Hi ~
Got your letter today ~ the
Army household sounds functional ~
Helene your bowling scores
aren't too good ~
It sounds cold state-side
If PX is at all efficient you
should have your x - mass gift
by the time of your
cocktail party ~ so open it ~
it'll be careful.

Boy I really have a great tape
collection going ~ people say
Piggy, swap tapes etc
I'll be getting a stereo cassette
player for you here ~ my hooch
mate ~ Bob Agust really, is getting
a combination reel (5½") + cassette
tape recorder ~ so I can
copy reels ~ Just befor I
DEROS ~ that means
leave this nice place ~ I'm
going to order a tape deck, amplifier

Complete Letter

5 NOV 70 THURS - 10:00 pm

Hi -

Got your letter today - the Parry household sounds functional -

Helene your bowling scores aren't good -
It sounds cold state-side

If PACEX is at all efficient you should have your Xmas gift by the time of your cocktail party - so open it n- it'll be <u>useful.</u>

Boy I really have a great tape collection going - people copy
- re-copy, swap tapes etc - I'll be getting a stereo cassette tape recorder for over here - my hooch mate - Bob Agustinelli is getting a combination reel (7 1/2") + cassette tape recorder - so I can copy feels - Just before I DEROS - that means leave this place - I'm going to order a tape deck, amplifier, turntable, speakers etc -

I've never heard such a beautiful sound as this stereo on tape - blows your mind.

Thank you for your first care package

Rainy and messy are right - but the sun actually showed today - first time in 10 days.

Do you smoke a lot Helene?

Cortisone can be bad news -

I've shown the kidnapping article to some other people here from MCV

4 minutes to extract an infant by C- section IS - FAST.

If you want to hear a tape or record to blow your mind - Listen to THE SEA by ROD McKUEN!

Snow shovels, EST, football games - sound great -

I look forward to letters from you all, Mom + Dad, Robin et al -

Thanks

I hate the FUCKING PLACE (That's French) Love
Eddie

Retrospective

News from the Perry household, bowling, and weather in Troy, MI.

The PACEX catalog, see line three, contained all sorts of duty-free goodies.

The acronym stands for Army & Air Force Exchange

Center. Again, the stereo equipment.

Care packages were exciting to receive and quickly devoured. Hickory Hill Farms meats and cheeses were a favorite.

The monsoons persisted.

Bob Agustinelli, my hooch mate, continued to fall asleep with his headphones on, so before I went to bed I would take them off and switch off the stereo. Bob died a few years ago from Agent Orange induced heart failure. My dear friend suffered for years and is the fourth herbicide/defoliant victim honored in this book.

Got on Helene for smoking.

We would deliver the Vietnamese mothers whose delivery progression ceased by C-section. A usual cause was the infant's head being too big to pass through the small Vietnamese pelvis if the father was an American.

I still listen to *The Sea.* A soothing, infectious, and romantic album. I did hate that fucking place! I did.

My sister Helene's birthday is on December 4th. I remembered.

The kidnapping reference pertained to fellow MCV trained physician. He was an internist serving in Vietnam. Hal Kushner, who grew up in Danville, Virginia, was the only American medical doctor held as a prisoner of war in Vietnam. Dr. Kushner served with the 1st Squadron, 9th US Cavalry, 1st Air Cavalry Division in Vietnam. He was captured on 2 December 1967 west of Tam Ky, South Vietnam, and released to American Control in Hanoi on 16 March 1973.

22 November 1970

Complete Letter

22 Nov '70

Hi Helene Jim

Happy Birthday Helene - too bad you didn't send me a card to send you -

Got your newsy letter today - with the letter from 1962 ~ 9 year ago to the day - I'm a little foggy - I passed that letter from Willie around - we all got a kick out of it - you know at first - when I saw the Richmond letterhead it thru me - after a while I couldn't believe it.

I sure you all had a good time Thanksgiving - We - that i Bob I he's the internist I share the hooch with - 2 private room - well I'll get smashed on Manhattans then some Very Cold Duck I found in the PX ($2.00 a bottle) - booze is CHEAP

I'm leaving for Saigon NOV 30 - to take my boards on Dec 2nd - I haven't studied worth a damn - I can't seem to get down to it - but I figure it'd accumulated knowledge - I hope - I have read some - I'll be there Dec 4th -

Glad to get the note from Jim - golf champ dig it (I'm picking up the EM (enlisted man) talk - also love beads and all

Skiing a lot of fun - I hear - since I can't - so is the lodge afterwards

-Soon I'll have to write you @ your office - especially after Saigon Take

care
Eddie

Retrospective

My sister Helene's birthday is on December 4th. I actually remembered. Another newsy letter appreciated.

Referencing the 1962 letter, Willie was on the waterfront staff at Camp Baiting Hollow with me when I was director and developed a crush on my sister, Helene.

Again, the reference to self-medicating. Since the PX was tax free, the liquor we purchased was dirt cheap. We enjoyed bourbon and coke, Bloody Mary's, and Crown Royal on the rocks.

The Army stopped the war for fellow surgeon **Charlie Carroll** and I to hitchhike on C-130's from Phu Bai to Saigon to take the written portion of our surgical board qualification exam. This test was being given in the states and around the world to all board candidates. The exam was on December 2nd. We departed on November 30th with the excuse that missing the exam was not an option. We were experts in getting on C-130's stand-by and knew we would have a few days before the exam to enjoy Saigon's French restaurants, especially the Le Cave, and the bars along Tu Do Street. A few days after the exam were also added.

On the night prior to the exam Charlie and I were wandering Tu Do street in our fatigues with the medical caduceus on our left lapel and a major's gold leaf on the right side. A very professional skinny black MP politely stopped us and inquired to see our military ID and ration card (for buying liquor). We were a little tipsy and perhaps would have given the kid some sarcasm until we spotted the two huge linebacker sized MPs in their jeep. The polite MP returned from the jeep and told us we were good to go. I then asked him, "Why did you stop us?" He responded, "Frankly sirs you do not look old enough to be Majors or act like you are." I took that as a compliment! Despite of being hung over we both passed with flying colors.

Congratulations to the "Golf Champ." Growing

up on Long Island, NY, I never skied.

8 December 1970

Hi Helen + Jim

Yes, it's still raining. I love your friend Rod McKuen — "The Sea" — it's a beautiful tape — but he does a bit called "Rain" — "I'll be glad if I never see it again" —

Sounds like you all had a nice Thanksgiving — Not a short trip either — I had a great time in Saigon — ate French food — beautiful restaurants — dinner — oh yeah — I was broken from — Saigon though it took me! I hope your Christmas gift gets there on time — get it for your party.

We're still stopping casualties — really tying — do a good job — People in Saigon don't

Complete Letter

8 DEC 70 WED

Hi Helene + Jim

Ye it's still raining. Have you heard Rod McKuen - "The Sea" - it's a beautiful tape - but he does a bit called "Rain" - "I'll be glad to never see it again" -YAH

Sounds like you all had a nice Thanksgiving - Not a bad trip either -

I had a great time in Saigon - ate French food, beautiful restaurants

- drank - Oh yeh - I also took an exam - I guess though it took me! I

hope your Christmas gift gets there on time
Open it for your party

We're still taking casualties- booby traps do a good job - People

in Saigon don't believe the war is going on -

The 3rd Field Hospital - an Army hospital- is just like state side - clean OR"S, nurses wear white. Here - we go into the OR in combat boots + fatigue pants with a crib shirt - JUST LIKE "MASH" - Phu bai is it to a "T" - only difference is that we live in a shanty.

Got your cards - thankx also got the gift of food etc - Have the holly piece hanging from the ceiling

Only 17 shopping days to Christmas- Bob Hope will be here Christmas day - maybe I can get on TV

Love Eddie

Retrospective

The monsoons continue.

Monsoon Season

"Yes, I'll be glad if I never see it (rain) again."

Getting out of Phu Bai to take my written portion of my surgical boards in Saigon was a joy. We made the most of our time there. I knew I did well on the exam.

The wounded kept on coming. The ingenious VC improvised the devastating booby traps to take advantage of the American lack of total commitment to the war. Our country was giving up and who wanted to be the last to die in this God forsaken place.

The Vietnam War, in '70-'71, was essentially over for those in Saigon but became more active as one traveled north. The 3rd Field Hospital was a state-side replica. The nurses wore pressed white outfits compared to sweaty fatigues and scrub outfits at the 85th. Our situation was identical to "M*A*S*H," except we lived in plywood shanties.

Those in Saigon who played in the Black Market did well.

I Corps, the most northern portion of South Vietnam in which Phu Bai resided, was very active.

The Third Field Hospital in Saigon did mostly elective surgery wherein the 85th Evac. treated fifty percent of the wounded.

All the troops in Vietnam were excited to see their base's **Bob Hope Show.**

1 January 1971

1 JAN 71

Hi there —
We had a joyous Christmas
holiday + New Year — artillery sr.?
x-mas eve a US ~~saturday~~
round hit a platoon of our
own men — killing 9
outright — sending 9 to us
for surgery + 15 to the aid
station — 2 of the pts. we
operated on have died since —
real nice war?

Got loaded — ill & just
nity — and Bobs & c
other sat around going —
the couple from grey Mom
+ Dad + Bolen — thanks
for the tape — you must have
give Mom + Dad a hint c
theirs

Glad you got your gift
before Christmas — not all
of them got there on time
— I steel don't know
which ones did arrive.

Complete Letter

1 Jan 71 Hi

there -
We had a joyous Christmas holiday + New Year -

X-Mass eve a US artillery round hit a platoon of our OWN men - killing 9 out right - sending 9 to us for surgery + 15 to the aid station - 2 of the pts we operated on have died since - real nice huh?

Got loaded ~ 11:00 pm that nite - and Bob I with others sat around opening - the care pkg from you, Mom + Dad + Robin _ Thank for the tape - you must have given Mom + Dad a hint with theirs

Glad you got your gift before Christmas - not all of them got there on time - I still don't know which ones did arrive.

This is the most depressing God damn place around any holiday
- last nite people got stoned sick trying to be happy - I drank, Ti Ti (Vietnamese for little) cause I had to re-operate on a guy this am -

Well 4 months down - 8 to go———!

I've taken some trips - a jeep to Hue took lots of pictures - a LOACH (small chopper) to Da Nang - flew over the Hi Van pass where all the trucks etc get ambushed blown up by the VC -

Not all that much really new - same old shit - rain, wounded, booze, choppers, etc.

I'll get all the match books I can - I wouldn't mind seeing even a messy stripper!

Hope your kids and you did have a nice holiday -

Oh yeh - Bob Hope came here a few days before X-Mass - shook his hand - big deal, huh?

See you sometime, Eddie

Retrospective

"Camp Eagle was a dusty diesel-fuel-exhaust-suffused ride in the back of a deuce and a half thirty minutes north of the 85th Evac. There appeared a makeshift stage with musicians, sound technicians, and stagehands scurrying around. MPs directed the human flow and protected the stage area. Since we accompanied our light-blue pajama- clad patients, we were in the preferred seats closer to the stage.

I had sworn to myself in the spirit of self-preservation not to participate in this event for there would be at least a couple thousand or more unarmed troops closely packed in one small area. What a great target for the VC. But that day was part of history, and I was drawn in.

Bob Hope should be sainted by our progressive Pope Francis; he was the greatest of men dedicating decades visiting American troops fighting in foreign countries without a hint of impatience or dwindling empathy. In the 85th Evac ICU, I was inches away from him and was struck by the true compassion he related to our wounded he visited.

At each base visited, he adapted his monologue to engage the troops by referencing their outfit, location, and commanding officers. He wore fatigue jackets and caps with the current unit's designations and toyed with his ever-present golf club.

Celebrities were always present with lesser known but stunning dancers. Jennifer Hosten (Miss World), Lola Falana, Ursula Andress, Les Brown and his Band of Renown, a twenty-two-year-old Johnny Bench, and the Gold Diggers were at Camp Eagle to entertain us."

Excerpted from my memoir *Welcome Home From Vietnam, Finally,*
Chapter: *Bob Hope Show*

The Bob Hope Show at Camp Eagle (not far from the 85th) was a huge event. Several thousand (looked that way) troops gathered on a sloping hill to watch the renowned performer. I was originally hesitant to go, fearing that such a large group of soldiers would be a prime target of the enemy.

Since we accompanied the blue pajama clad patients we got seated next to the stage. There were stretchers, wheelchairs, and fluids running in from IV poles. The audience was awash with cheer and excitement. Bob did his monologue referencing the 101st Airborne and its leaders.

A very young Johnny Bench, the renowned catcher, Miss World, and the Ding a Lings, a young female song and dance group from the Dean Martin Show, all participated to the crowd's pleasure. Our hospital commander, Colonel Sugiyama, invited the troop to visit the 85th Evac. patients. Our helipad was just big enough to accommodate the large C-46, Chinook helicopter, and was allowed to land.

Mr. Hope did not shy away from the mutilated kids and embraced each one with sincere best wishes.

The show's women were a great hit with the patients and were totally engaging. The lead singer of the Ding a Lings from the Dean Martin Show sang to one of my patients.

I photographed her and entitled the photo a "Christmas Angel." These young women were about the same age of the fighting men. They risked injury and death flying around Vietnam over enemy forces - I feel that they qualify as Vietnam veterans.

In NYC, an Army veteran friend of mine, **Martin Edelman,** to whom I had given my memoir, viewed that photo, recognized her, and introduced us a few years ago. Her name is **Michelle DellaFave,** and she continues to perform. She is an ardent supporter of New York City Veterans and Manhattan's VVA Chapter 126.

We expected the war to quiet down during the Christmas season. The enemy did seem to back off. A fitting celebration was planned for Christmas Eve. **Duane Wall** , an OR medic specialist, had been involved in organizing the evening's festivities.

Instead, we participated in a Christmas Eve mass casualty disaster. The true story of how it occurred is a matter of debate. A newbie Lieutenant may have called in his position (coordinates) as an enemy target for the firing of American high explosive artillery from afar. The other theory reflects that the area of operations was too crowded with American troops and another platoon mistakenly called in the deadly artillery strike.

Either way, nine were killed outright and fifteen were wounded. Of the latter three were hemorrhaging profusely and taken straight to the OR. In two kids the bleeding could not be controlled, and they died in the operating room. One was my patient. The third grunt died post-operatively. That's twelve dead adolescents due to a "mistake." Yes, more to be *buried.*

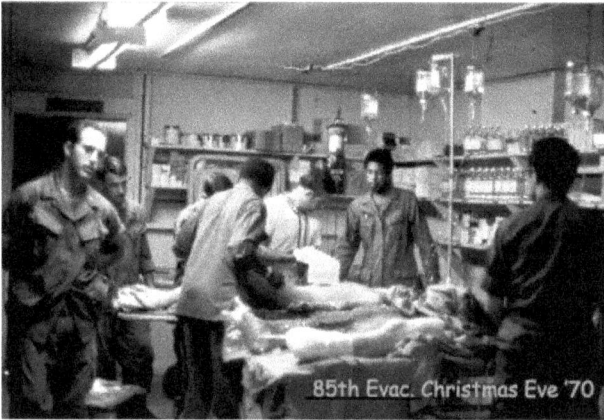

Christmas Eve 1970 mass casualty wounded. Trauma surgeon, Charlie Caroll right, and orthopedic surgeon Leo Flynn, white t-shirt in center

Other wounded grunts with open (protruding through the skin) extremity fractures and traumatic amputations were relieved because their wounds had saved their lives and they were going home!

One soldier who just happened to sit with his back to a large tree stump was shielded from the deadly shrapnel and survived without a scratch. He continues to suffer PTSD and survivor guilt.

"This is the most depressing Goddamn place around any holiday."

That Christmas Eve our routine of post trauma *self-medicating* with alcohol began at 11:00 pm. - "last nite people got stoned sick trying to be happy." At least I restricted my drinking that night knowing I had surgery the next morning.

This next story reflects a deficit in my brain's executive function reflected in diminished common sense and increased risk taking.

"A few of us escaped the 85th compound to embark on the dangerous trip South on Highway 1 headed for the Da Nang PX to buy tomato juice. There was none to be had at the 85th.

One of the favorite drinks on the non-bunker-bunker was the Bloody Mary. There were no state or federal taxes on the booze purchased in the PX (Post Exchange). Great brand names of all types of medicinal liquids were inexpensive. I still enjoy Crown Royal forty-six years later.

The challenge presented as an acute shortage of tomato juice! None was hoarded or in the PX and the usually tuned-in sergeants were stumped. Drastic action was indicated. We would drive south an hour or so to the Da Nang PX and make a reviving purchase. However, for us to succeed, several obstacles had to be addressed: our prohibition to drive in the country, an international driver's license, a vehicle, and our safety as we drove in an open jeep and traversed the often-crowded Hai Van Pass.

I went to the base motor pool and bartered with a mechanic I knew for the international driver's test and answers. After a brief study session, we were administered the test and passed.

The docs were not supposed to have weapons, but as patients were brought into the ED, they were separated from their M16s, Thompson submachine guns, and M79 grenade launchers. Somehow, a few of those weapons found their way into our possession.

Since the deficit in tomato juice availability persisted, four of us reaffirmed our commitment to our non-bunker-bunker brothers. Early one morning we departed the 85th in our stolen jeep for Da Nang.

We turned south on Highway 1. Speeding along to avoid becoming a sniper's target the beautiful countryside flashed by. We saw water buffalos, rice paddies, women in conical hats on the streets and toiling in the paddies, bare bottomed babies, small children, and ramshackle huts constructed with discarded wood and flattened beer and soda cans.

Continuing our drive the majestic shoreline of the South China Sea was on our left and the purple-green mountains to our right.

Driving uphill, behind a series of trucks, into the Hi Van Pass we readied our weapons since truck convoys are routinely sniped at with enemy small arms fire. Out of nowhere Cobra gunship helicopters screamed by and fired rockets into the threatening hillsides. Plumes of white-gray smoke postmarked our right flank. The sense of relief blanketed us when exiting the pass downhill.

Once over the pass, it was clear sailing to the Da Nang PX and an abundance of tomato juice with which to quench the 85th Evac's thirst for Bloody Mary's.

Da Nang city was bustling with people on motor bikes and walking. The PX was huge compared to Phu Bai's with a plethora of varied items at dirt cheap prices. After securing several cases of tomato juice I purchased a conical pearl ring for Robin.

The trip back to the 85th in the dark was uneventful. We did have two M16s, a Thompson and a M79 with plenty of ammunition - and no weapons training.

However, as we were experiencing the adventure in real time, there were occasions when we asked, **'What the hell are we doing?'** The jeep offered no protection except for continued forward motion. Since we never stopped, all my photos of that trip have a blurred foreground. Was there an enemy element that would decide to snipe at us? Would the traffic be backed up at the Hai Van Pass slowing us to a stop and making us sitting ducks? We were not shot at as far as I know. We made it back to the hospital compound without incident."

Excerpted from my memoir: *Welcome Home From Vietnam, Finally,*
Chapter: *Tomato Juice*

During the Vietnam War and all the Post 911 Wars, about twenty percent of the deaths were from non-hostile occurrences. That would be "accidents, attempted murder by a leader's men, 'friendly fire,' drownings, overdoses, suicides, MVAs, and horsing around. That would reflect over ten thousand of the dead listed on the Vietnam Veterans Memorial (the Wall) in Washington, DC. Why? Idle hands, loss of the fabric (discipline) of the Army, adolescence, alcohol, heroin, weed, evolving PTSD, and the accessibility of weapons.

There were the occasional murders on the compound. Everyone is armed with M16s, M79s (grenade launcher), or sidearms. Alcohol, heroin, the conflicting moral code of killing overwhelming that of peace, and the adolescent lack of control were the key ingredients.

One evening a cook was shot at close range with a M16. He was dying from a massive intra-abdominal hemorrhage. In the ED I opened his abdomen planning to clamp the aorta to stop the hemorrhage. I could not identify any major organs or vessels - they had been pulverized by the ballistic shock wave reflecting 6000 horsepower of energy from the bullet.

As the attending physician I was ordered to testify at the murder trial in Da Nang. I was told to drive down. Having risked that trip once for tomato juice I said I required a helicopter ride. Sure, enough a LOACH (OH-6 Cayuse) landed on our helipad. The Army utilized it to scout the enemy and draw their fire allowing the Cobra Gunships to target and destroy the VC and NVA.

My pilot was relieved to not be in combat with the assignment to ferry me about Vietnam. After spending an hour and a half testifying in Da Nang we flew up and down the East coast of Vietnam over the South China Sea visiting my friends at various evacuation hospitals.

A great day away from my usual Vietnam.

My LOACH for the day

Flooded Rice Paddies

Fishing Village

30 January 1971

30 JAN 71
SAT

Hi there.

Got a letter from you today
— 6 pages over - simplified —
got several things out of ready it

*① It's too damn cold to go
back to N.E - US to practice

*② I don't feel like screwing
around with this in the N.E. US.
winters

*③ — I do think your problem
is a problem

*④ I am in a cast - my
right leg - from playing
basketball at our "gym" —
a evulsed my plantar fascia
from its origin on the
calconeus — My aches ward
my right heel is F__K ED
up! — I feel sorry for Jim's eye

Complete Letter

30 JAN 71 SAT
Hi there

Got a letter from you today - 6 pages over - 2 wk period - got several things out of reading it

#1 It's too damn cold to go back to the N.E. - US to practice

#2 I don't feel like screwing around with cars in the N.E.U.S. winters

#3 I do think you® problem is a problem

#4 I am in a cast - my right leg - from playing basketball at our "gym" - avulsed my plantar fascia from its origin on the calcaneus - In other words my right heel is F_ KED up!

I feel sorry for Jim's eye

8 below zero - you can have it -

I went to Japan - 1 and 1/2 weeks ago - it's winter there too - froze my ass off in my summer uniform - but had a ball - got Jim lots of match books from several establishments.

I visited - toured the city - ate Kobe steak - the Japs massage the beast + feed it rice wine to keep the meat tender - it was -

Got your package - used the red ones as a joke last nite to play basketball and screwed up my goddamn leg up - the red blinded me + I tripped! - Thanks

They took a lot of movies at the 85th - i.e. the cameramen with Bob Hope - I understand no pictures of the hospital were on TV - of course not _ this place is a substandard place -

We're a bit tense up here - cause a huge American + ARVN force is gathering ~ 30 miles above us between Quang Tree (Tri) + the DMZ
- looks like a push into Laos - that means lots of OR time - Remember this date I'm writing + see if the push does occur how they describe it on the news

We hear there tanks side by side over ~ 30 miles facing Laos -

If we go there Nixon will not be challenging Congress + it will be a move to save Cambodia from falling -

This is Tet - the Vietnamese new year - May be some fireworks up here -

Talking to some pilots - so many bombs have been dropped on the "Trail" (Ho Chi Minh) that the jungle has turned into soft sand - the planes bomb and move the sand - Enemy bulldozers push it aside at night - the trucks rumble + we bomb again the next day - STUPID!

It'll be a sight operating in this damn cast

- See ya
Eddie

Retrospective

My responses to Helene's newsy letter were specific.

However, I eventually violated #1 and #2 since I lived and practiced surgery in Amsterdam, NY. Twenty-five miles west of the state's capital, Albany, this small city is located near the Mohawk River and just below the foothills of the beautiful Adirondack Mountains. Robin and I and the children did successfully accommodate the cold, driving in the winter, and "..screwing around with cars in the winter." Perhaps the biggest adjustment was for Brooklyn native Robin to adapt to living in such a rural environment. Her first observation was "There are no sidewalks." She adapted extremely well.

Our family flourished under Robin's guidance as my children and practice grew. In contrast to the stereotypical Brooklynite, she oversaw the care of our horses and became accomplished in loading and backing up the horse trailer - not an easy task.

Robin became involved in the community, concentrating on the future of the Amsterdam Free Library through fundraising and efficient guidance when serving as chairman of its board.

Before I departed for my service in Vietnam, due to the concentration required during surgical training, medicine and surgery were paramount. My residency buddy, Deming Payne, referred to our existence as "child abuse for adults."

In Vietnam I experienced the separation from family, the gift of downtime to evaluate life, and the witnessing of war's devastation on body, mind, and soul. I soon realized that **Robin, Kim,** and **Chris** were the paramount considerations. Therefore, I decided to not pursue academia but to commit to solo private practice in a small community, ie., Amsterdam. Mission accomplished!

I tore the plantar fascia on the sole of the right foot - it was painful.

A walking cast to the right lower leg and foot did relieve the pain and fostered healing. The injury occurred playing basketball in a building space we procured and renovated into a gym. A volleyball court was also delineated. It was one and a half feet short in length. We beat the Vietnamese teams (their favorite sport at that time) for their spikes were often "long."

The doctors rotated in accompanying the wounded as they were evacuated to Japan. This duty was a respite from the war and Vietnam. We would travel in our summer khakis by a C-130 equipped to transport patients to Saigon. The young soldiers were then transferred to a C-141 Starlifter for a flight to the Army hospital in Tachikawa, Japan. A short train ride to Tokyo presented a view of Mt. Fuji. At six-three in my uniform I towered over the Japanese riders. I realized WWII was just twenty-five years ago and my co-riders must have mixed emotions about my presence.

We would stay at the Army's Sanno Hotel in Tokyo. Our first responsibility was to visit the huge Tokyo PX and fulfill a shopping list for stereo and photographic items ordered by the 85th Evac staff. I was relieved to be rid of the five thousand or more in cash I was carrying. Most of the items were shipped back to the "world" - home.

I was then free to tour Tokyo and the surrounding countryside. I took the tram up to Mount Mitake and wandered around stoned. All my photos were blurred by movement due to smoking weed. The Kobe steak was delicious! I stayed as long as I dared but in the process of partying for days I lost my shot record. That folded yellow document was essentially my passport to re-enter Vietnam and return to the 85th on a timely basis and avoid being AWOL. I visited Tachikawa Hospital and persuaded a young charge nurse to forge me a new shot record.

Hitchhiking on C-130s back to Phu Bai from Saigon, I encountered one of our nurses, Jeanie. At the Da Nang airport we were surrounded by young, traumatized grunts. She asked me to guard the door of the nearest latrine as she made her urgent entrance.

My effort was successful. What a gentleman.

10 FEB 71
~ 930p

Hi there –
Got your card today –
completely undamaged – Aced
it + ate it with the
help of a number of hungry
guys. Thank you –
By now I guess Jim has
made his mind up concerning
his big move. I'm sure
it'll work out – sure has
so far.
In about 9 days I leave
for R+R – man, its going
to be great seeing Robin again
still be 6 months – wow
I don't really believe the
Goddamn army has sent

Complete Letter

10 Feb 71

9:30 PM

Got your cake today -completely <u>undamaged</u> - Iced it + ate it with the help of a number of hungry guys. Thank you -

By now I guess Jim has made his mind up concerning his big move. I'm sure it'll work out - sure has so far.

In about 9 days I have R&R - man it's going to be great seeing Robin again. It'll be 6 months -

Wow, I don't really believe the God damn Army has sent me over here - Oh well 6 to go then it's over - I always thought the Army was worthless - now I know it is.

Liked your card too - WE haven't been busy at all - the Vietnamese are invading Laos - the GIs backing them up. But if the sun stays out like today we'll get busy for sure -easier to count your dead -Better picture for the news papers too-

Bitter - me - never -

Well be good - I going to have a blast in Hawaii Love
Eddie

What a wonderful surprise!

I visited the mail room a few days after my birthday and was presented with a mid-sized box covered with shipping paper. The return address was Helene's.

With Bob, my roommate, observing, I carefully opened my package. The contents emitted the order of a cake. Two aluminum wrapped baked cake layers appeared with a can of Hershey's chocolate icing. Everything was fresh, moist, and intact after traveling eight thousand miles over a five-day period - in and out of several aircraft.

My brother-in-law, Jim, was considering an executive position change with a new company.

He did make the move and was extremely successful.

American casualties were fewer due the heavy monsoons and the ARVNs doing most of the fighting in Laos.

Once the sun reappeared the generals would resume sending grunts to die in a war that the United States was deserting.

"By February 1971, I had not seen Robin for almost six months. We had communicated by mail, tape reels, and the MARS line. My son, Chris, addressed Robin's tape recorder as daddy for that was where my voice emanated.

This pacific reunion could have been a marital disaster. We had led disparate lives, endured unique challenges, and become self-sufficient in our separate circumstances. Our seamless engagement of the new us was not dictated by marriage vows but by the fact we had been friends for years before we wedded.

Kim was five and had demanded to see her daddy. Robin did not want to share her time with me, so she told Kim the generals did not allow children in Hawaii. My daughter accepted her fate until she later noticed, after Robin's return, children in the newly developed R&R photos. An awkward discussion followed.

Robin had arrived a day early and attempted to register in the Hilton Rainbow Towers but there had been a clerical error. The hotel compensated by upgrading us to an elegant suite on the fifteenth floor.

She then enjoyed our balcony and the hotel's pool and beach. Later that day, she visited the Honolulu WASAMA Chapter.

An uncomfortable military bus then shepherded our psyched and recently de-planed group to Fort Derussy, an R&R facility on Waikiki beach, to check us in, inform us of local regulations, and provide the VD lecture.

The army had also driven the wives to Derussy.

Robin looked great!

The suite itself was amazing, but its best feature was privacy in a bathroom equipped with a flushing toilet!

From our balcony, Diamond Head loomed a few miles away against a royal blue sky.

The weather was perfect. The time was bittersweet for we had to separate again, but we enjoyed being together.

The Rainbow Towers Hotel view was of Waikiki Beach with Diamond Head in the background. The sand was clean, deep, and welcoming. The water was warm, clear, and sea green (can't escape green).

There was also a pool located near the hotel directly below our fifteenth-story balcony. While relaxing at the poolside, I was experimenting with my telephoto lens and informed Robin that I could read the Kahlua label clearly on our balcony. After observing all the GIs with their cameras, she issued an embarrassed gasp for she had been on the balcony scantily clad the day before improving her tan.

One day, we rented a white MG Midget and with the top-down drove east along the coast. As we progressed the topography became a lush green countryside.

The highways we utilized have been altered over the years, but I remember climbing over the aged volcanic rock at the Halona Blowhole and having a delightful lunch at the Lion's Head Inn.

There were fishermen along the coast skillfully throwing fine nets to trap their prey. We visited a surfing beach. The surf was not up, but we enjoyed walking on the damp sand.

We then diverted to the west and passed immense pineapple fields that extended to the horizon.

Heading south and east, we returned past the Arizona Memorial to Honolulu and the Rainbow Towers, which is shown at the beginning of the Hawaii Five-O TV show.

Another day, we traveled to the Polynesian Cultural Center, which defined the Hawaiian cultural and historical background.

We dined at a few fine restaurants within walking distance of the Hilton.

Then there was the obligatory luau, huge crowds, drinks, hula dancing, comedian, and pig roast.

To this day, I believe the MC on stage reflected the island's exhaustion of having GIs disrupting their lives, culture, and city despite of all the dollars that were flowing into Oahu. He used the term "haole" incessantly to address his audience.

The word refers to a white man or foreigner, but with a change in intonation, it becomes a most derogatory term. My turn to be referred to with disdain. The young kids and their wives and girlfriends had no understanding of the racist slur and laughed at his every word. I was pissed!

We then departed paradise."

Excerpt from my memoir *Welcome Home From Vietnam, Finally,* Chapter: *R&R*

6 mar ?
~ 9³⁰ pm

Hi there,

Well it's back to Plei Bai
We had a great time in AR
stayed in a beautiful hotel.
Took lots of pictures with my
camera equipment —
Hey Jim — this camera
a Minolta is easy to use +
takes great pictures —
cost ~ $350 in the states —
Cost me $130 — I plan to
get rid of it when I get down
to the World (I'm getting
a new camera in Hong Kong) —
I'll sell it to you at cost
if you want it — nothing
wrong with it — I just
want a new one — let
me know — Robin

Complete Letter

6 MAR 71

~ 9:30 pm Hi

there,

Well it's back to Phu Bai. We had a great time on R&R - stayed at a beautiful hotel. Took lots of pictures with my camera equipment -

Hey Jim - this camera a Minolta is easy to use + takes great pictures - cost ~ $350 in the states - cost me $131.00 - I plan to get rid of it when I get back to the World (I'm getting a new camera in Hong Kong) - I'll sell it to you at cost if you want it - nothing wrong with it - I just want a new one - let me know -Robin can bring it home from Hong Kong - <u>duty free</u>. Take a look at the pictures I took in Hawaii -

We're Phu Bai champs in volleyball + basketball (no help from me with my foot) - it's better now

We begin softball practice tomorrow + then to the ocean for the afternoon - War is hell - Why not! -

I'm taping now - just put Best of the Animals, Cowslips in Concert, Crosby, Stills, Nash and Young, Rolling Stones + Iron Butterfly - In - A

- Da - Vita - are all real <u>Heavy!</u> Well

be good

I think I'll get drunk

Eddie

Back in Phu Bai.

No more "flush toilets" until I meet Robin and Kim in Hong Kong.

I tried again to sell a Minolta SRT 101 to Jim. He never did take me up on my offer - even offered to have Robin bring it home from Hong Kong.

"With the sun shining, the sky clear, and the heat rising, a perfect solution was a trip to the beach. Phu Bai was not far from the east coast and the South China Sea. On weekends, we boarded a CH-47 Chinook helicopter for the short trip over unsettled territory to Eagle Beach. There were steel plates on the deck of the chopper to deflect small arms fire. Up front, a crewman on the port-side manned an M60 machine gun.

Interest in volleyball and basketball subsided. Softball practices were beginning with Casey Blitt, our anesthesiologist, and Fred Brockschmidt, a Regular Army captain nurse anesthetist, organizing and coaching. After practice we would load up on Chinook (CH-47) and be taxied to Eagle Beach.

CH-47 Chinook Helicopter

After walking up the CH-47 ramp we sat along the fuselage in webbed jump seats with our towels, suntan lotion, and refreshments - a bit incongruous for a war zone. Upon liftoff, we could look out the rear of the chopper and watch the airport, and its aircraft diminish in size.

That same transient feeling of doom one experiences today on a commercial flight in the United States passed through me, slightly magnified, every time I flew in choppers.

Eagle Beach was designated by the military as an in-country Rest & Relaxation (R&R) destination for the troops. At times, there were hundreds of GIs fresh from the boonies, both enlisted and officers. The new variable our arrival introduced were our feminine nurses. The ladies stayed close to us but were totally engaging when approached by an admiring trooper.

The water temperature was perfect and the waves moderate. We were cautioned about poisonous sea snakes, but no one was ever bitten. The sand was grayish white, deep, warm, and relaxing. With my eyes closed and the sun beaming down on me, I drifted back into my Hampton Bays, Long Island, New York, high school summer days."

Excerpted from my memoir, *Welcome Home From Vietnam, Finally:*

Chapter *Lighter Side..*

Again, "I think I'll get drunk."

I was burying more pain.

29 May 1971

29 may 71

Hi y'all

[illegible handwritten letter]

Complete Letter

29 MAY 71

Hi y'all

I'm in the chapel now - taping - it's air-conditioned and there is little static in the electricity - therefore few "clicks' on the tapes we copy
- We sent away to Taipei - - for $4:00 - and this is illegal because of copyright laws - you get 3 hr tape with 5 albums on it - actually a $20 - $30 value

We ordered ~ 50 tapes - 4 of us and now we just copy the ones we want - I ordered 20 for myself + will copy another 9 or 10 - that means I'll come home with ~ 65 - 3 hour tapes - all kinds - rock, acid, popular, old, country + western, classical.

I'm really looking forward to hearing this stuff on my stereo equipment - I've ordered.

Sorry I haven't written sooner-I'm getting SHORT - I'll be a two digit midget on 31 May

- 99 days left in this Goddamn place -

In a few days I'll be with Robin + Kim in HK + BK. When I get back it'll be 74 days to go _ I'll break that up with a trip to Japan.

I just read MASH - you should- it's a bit more realistic that the movie + relates well our feelings, our actions + thoughts

Don't worry about the Pap - an infection can give you a suspicious smear - anyway that's WHY you have a pap done anyway - to pick up a problem very <u>early</u> - Right _ right

I'm glad Jim's enjoying his new company - I've got a lot to talk to him about when I get back -

Love Ed.

Retrospective

What a dichotomy, using the chapel to tape reel to reel music and not to pray. The air conditioning and more stable electrical current were all the enticement I needed.

The illegal market for music thrived in Southeast Asia. We copied all genres of music for hours - it kept us busy and distracted us from the war and wounded. We would ship thirty to forty "seven inch" reels of music back to the "World" when DEROS arrived.

Becoming "short" had nothing to do with stature - it meant that you had less than one-hundred days left in Vietnam's living hell. I would be a "two-digit midget" with seventy-four days left when I returned from Hong Kong and Bangkok after visiting Robin and Kim, my five-year-old daughter.

The book *and* movie *M*A*S*H* about the Korean War closely mimicked our experience at the 85th Evac. But we lived in hooches, and they survived in tents.

The Women by Kristin Hannah is the most accurate representation of our life at the 85th Evac. that I've found. This book also precisely exposes the main character, Frankie's, descent into PTSD and attempted suicide. In fact, the number of attempted suicides in the military and veteran groups far out-number the fatalities.

FYI:

As reported by Reuters in February 2013, there were at that time twenty- two active-duty military personnel and veterans from Vietnam and the Post 911 wars killing themselves each day. That translates to approximately one every sixty-five minutes.

More than sixty-nine percent of veteran suicides occur in veterans fifty years or older...a majority served in Vietnam and have for decades been suffering progressively severe PTSD.

In recent decades approximately 1.7 million men and women have served in Iraq, Afghanistan, and peripheral conflicts. With the accumulative exposures of redeployment, there is a major upward impact on the incidence of PTSD, prescription opioid and alcohol abuse, smoking, and suicide; in each category the incidence in the military exceeds that of the general public.

Sixty-eight percent of active-duty military suicides
were thirty years old or younger, for their brains
are more adolescent than mature.

Is there an explanation for this inconceivable travesty?

Yes, there is! Please watch:

Confronting Military PTSD and Suicide: https://youtu.be/ajT9-LOF6R8?si=3df-jI9KA9De6DtN

Helene was told she had a precancerous Pap cervical smear. Obviously, she at age twenty-seven was concerned. She eventually underwent hysterectomy surgery. Today a cone biopsy, removing the abnormal cervical cells would be the initial treatment.

I was counting the days until I joined Robin and Kim in Hong Kong.

Getting "short" led to teenage-like behavior.

"Roger's surgical abilities were unassailable, but he harbored one haunting fear when at the 85th Evac. That challenge was having to perform an appendectomy on a specific doc. Bob, as you know, was my roommate, but you may not realize he was a very big man. Roger dreaded a surgical encounter with Bob.

One evening after we all had consumed a few bourbons and cokes, I left the O Club for about a half hour and returned to present Roger with the news that Bob had appendicitis. He quickly responded that he'd be happy to assist me at Bob's surgery. I pleaded with him that Bob and I were so close I would feel more comfortable if he assumed the responsibility of Bob's care. All he could say was "oh shit" repetitively.

Now, as you may have surmised, this illness was a complete fabrication. I had coached Bob on the signs and symptoms of acute appendicitis and how to physically respond to Roger's abdominal examination. The ED, OR, corpsmen, docs, and essentially everyone on the compound knew that Bob's illness was bogus. We even created lab results to reinforce the diagnosis. In the ED, a half-empty IV bottle was hung, and its needleless end was taped to his forearm.

An empty antibiotic solution bag dangled from the IV pole. It was a long walk from the Club to the ED for Roger. He kept shaking his head and exclaiming "oh no" repeatedly. To his chagrin upon completing his examination, Roger was convinced Bob did have acute appendicitis and required immediate surgery.

Bob was wheeled to the OR and placed on the table; his abdomen washed, painted with iodine solution, and draped. Roger stepped into the room, preparing himself mentally for the imminent challenge, and nodded at Bob, who sat up, nimbly jumped off the table, and said, "I'm going back to the club." The entire gathering erupted with laughter. Roger became very quiet. I could see a range of emotion flash across his face from anger to relief to 'they got me.' Roger was able to go home without having to operate on Bob. Indeed, at our 85th Evac reunion in 2014, the bogus patient still had his appendix."

Excerpted from my memoir, *Welcome Home From Vietnam, Finally,*
Chapter: *Lighter Side*

7 July 1971

7 July 71

Hi there,

Well we just had a
typhoon — blew the roof of
the O-club supply + other
hootches — building fell off
their stilts — OR flooded —
I said F — it and
started drinking ~12 then
yesterday — had a typhoon
party + got very blown
away myself. Everything
is quiet today.

Copper may know we
will live 2 surgeons at
the 85th for the past 2½
wks — the other guys
a few who is supposed to
be fully trained

Complete Letter

7 July,71 Hi

there,

Well we just had a typhoon - blew off the roof of the O-Club, supply and other hooches - buildings fall off their stilts - OR flooded -

I said F—K it and started drinking ~12:00 noon yesterday - had a typhoon party + got very blown away myself. Everything is quiet today -

As you may know we've had 2 surgeons at the 85th for the past 2 1/2 weeks - the other guy is supposed to be fully trained but can't operate for shit - and needs me to make decisions for him - so essentially I'm on straight everyday - the stupid Army sends people home without replacing them - in the long run the GI suffers - but what's a couple dead kids more - right!

Haven't gotten a letter from your GYN man yet. Glad you're feeling better- I still think you should have a hysterectomy within the year - no rush - but you don't fool around with abnormal pathology - Thinking like a surgeon not a brother -I like to be as 100% as I can and that's a hysterectomy

We had a great trip - I got some great clothes. Robin rings etc - It was nice having my first family with me - meeting Chris and learning to know him will be an experience -

Thanks for the article on the pool - it was at the 85th

Sgt. Balance got back a few days ago 61 days

in VN

57 days left in Phu Bai

Back again -

Just cleaned my 38 - I feel better when it's in working order.

See ya in Sept,

Love

Eddie

Retrospective

The typhoons in Southeast Asia, where Vietnam is located, are equivalent to hurricanes we experience in the eastern United States. The loosely applied corrugated metal roofs of our plywood structures were easily lifted by the winds. Of most concern was the missing roof from our "O" Club; the sickly green plywood elevated shanty we frequented.

All buildings were on two-foot stilts except the ED, OR's, and the Recovery Room/ICU. They were built on concrete slabs at ground level and were not ditched. All these areas predictably flooded, and we worked in two to three inches of red- brown water. We dug aggressively to ditch the structures and avoid further damage. The brilliant Army Corps of Engineers should have thought to ditch the buildings when they were built.

Eventually, as the flow of wounded ended, we used the typhoon as an excuse to resume drinking - even calling our activity a "Typhoon Party." This was "self-medicating" to **bury** the repetitive ugliness of war.

The Army was pulling away from I Corps, the most northern section of South Vietnam close to the DMZ, where my hospital was located. In doing so, troops of the 101st Airborne were being withdrawn. The powers that be predicted fewer wounded in our area of service since the pursuit of the enemy was becoming increasingly limited. But we were still relatively busy with wounded kids.

Our number of surgeons was reduced from four to two. It was just me and a surgeon who was useless despite being advertised as fully trained. He was incapable of good judgement and operating effectively without me holding his hand. So, for two and a half months I was on 24/7. It was tiring. Our current causality volume required at least three competent trauma surgeons.

So, what if more kids die due to the Army's position that the troops were expendable. To fill my new role, I had to be a more conservative drinker. I had some judgement remaining.

I was waiting for input from Helene's doctor concerning my sister's abnormal Pap smear. I again advised her to undergo hysterectomy.

I have no recollection of Sgt. Balance.

Several times a day we would applaud ourselves at being "Short."

Doctors were not issued weapons. Although we all had them - M16s, Thompson Submachine Guns, 38 pistols, and 45 semi autos. We stole the guns from patients who arrived in the ED before the MPs could sequester them.

"A loaded 38 holstered revolver hung at the head of my bed, hopefully never to be used. There had been occasional attempted intrusions of the compound's perimeter by the Viet Cong (VC). It was reported to us that Vietnamese locals who had worked on the compound by day were killed at the wire at night. These sappers carried explosives hoping to slither through the encircling protective sharp-edged Concertina wire (improved barbed wire) to blow up personnel sleeping in their hooch's. One did not enter another's hooch without announcing your presence for you could be shot."

Excerpted from my memoir *Welcome Home From Vietnam, Finally,*
Chapter: *Home Sweet Home*

Robin, Kim, and I had a wonderful trip to Hong Kong and Bangkok. We flew into Hong Kong to spend a week in both countries. Robin and Kim arrived a day early from the US via Los Angeles, Honolulu, and Tokyo.

"As my aircraft negotiated its landing at the old Hong Kong Airport, I was certain we would land in the harbor's waters. Robin and I had both arrived a day early.

I checked in at the Hong Kong Hotel's desk, asked for my wife, and was directed to the dining room. As I entered in my khaki uniform, I heard a high pitched five-year-old girl scream from across the room. There followed running footsteps and the heart-wrenching shout, 'Daddy, Daddy, I have not seen you in a year.' There was not a dry eye in the restaurant as she jumped into my arms and squeezed my neck. When Robin arrived at the scene, she was asked if she was not jealous. 'Of course not,' she replied.

That afternoon, Kim lost her first baby tooth in the room. The tooth fairy placed a Hong Kong dollar under her pillow during the night."

Excerpt from my memoir; *Welcome Home From Vietnam, Finally.*
Chapter: *Short Timer*

Hong Kong Harbor,1971, from Victoria Peak

Robin and I decided Kim should experience a rickshaw ride. Well, the old man took off running and we chased after them worried about the abduction of our child.

We chose a Hong Kong tailor. Robin and I were ordering a truck- load of inexpensive clothes to be made from his shop. Therefore, he willingly guided us around the city and surrounding area. We took the tram up Victoria Peak and viewed Tiger Balm Gardens. Inland we visited Aberdeen.

The next day it was the New Territories at Hong Kong's border with China.

I was fascinated that high-rise construction was completed using only thick bamboo tubes as scaffolding.

It was then on to Bangkok and its wonders.

"Upon arriving in Bangkok, we chose to hire a driver for the week at the going eighty-dollar rate. He would be available day or night and was always in close proximity. He was our tour guide and protector.

What a colorful city. I remember pointed, elongated, and extremely colorful upside-down ice cream cone-shaped crowns on all the ancient buildings. There were short staircases and twisting pathways negotiating the multicolored sandcastle-appearing buildings. Dark gray reliefs scattered throughout the beautiful buildings reminded the visitor of the monkey people and Thailand's warrior history.

There were numerous Buddhas to discover. The Reclining Buddha was indeed reclining under an open-sided roofed structure. It was massively long, and the gold leaf had peeled off in large sections, revealing the dullness below.

The Golden Buddha was indeed a golden color. It is related that to fool invaders centuries ago, it was covered with concrete and only in recent history was the hidden treasure discovered. I recall my pious Catholic daughter kneeling with solemnly bowed head praying to the Golden Buddha."

Excerpt from my memoir; *Welcome Home From Vietnam, Finally*, Chapter: *Short Timer*

Robin and Kim in Bangkok

We explored the Chao Phraya River and its tributaries in a colorfully decorated outboard watercraft powered by a car engine and long drive shaft to adapt to shallow waters.

That fall, back in school, Kim's teacher asked the class what they had done over the summer. Kim stood and informed the class that she went around the world. She had, for their return flight, went eastward to arrive in JFK.

The teacher replied, 'in your dreams.' Kim countered that she was on a boat in Bangkok that went into a small river and there were wooden boats with fruit and flies on the fruit. The teacher responded that she now believed Kim.

Read Chapter *Short Time* r in my memoir *Welcome Home From Vietnam, Finally,* for a full description of our stay in both cities.

Upon returning to the 85th, I was a two-digit midget with sixty-one days left in Vietnam.

I continued making evening rounds i.e., visiting my post-op patients. Most would be evacuated to Saigon, Okinawa, Japan, or the US by the next day.

I never learned their names. It never entered my mind; efficient
burying.

A name I will never forget is Sgt. Richard Barbee whose injury and surgery was the most horrific I've ever experienced.

**My mental Waterloo in Vietnam resulted by
chance because of the on-call list.**

Sometime in early March 1971 at midday, I was summoned to the ED for a solitary wounded American. An IV with Ringer's Lactate (salt solution) was infusing. His torso was covered by blankets, but they seemed empty where his legs should have been. He had been given some blood in the field.

He had been chosen to be decimated when the VC triggered the explosion of a command detonated salvaged US anti-tank mine as his patrol passed by the concealed enemy.

He was totally alert, oriented, communicative and rational. And he was very much alive.

His blood pressure, pulse, temperature, and urinary output were totally normal. His wounds were not bleeding. Yet he had suffered the worst booby trap injury I had ever witnessed, been told about, or could imagine.

His legs were traumatically amputated below his destroyed thighs, his perineum was split open, his genitalia were gone, and mud, dirt, and debris were blasted into his lower body.

By our triage standards, was he expectant or salvageable? Should I hide him from the world and infuse him with perhaps too much morphine and hasten his death? That in my mind would have been murdering this very much alive man and condemning him to a non-dignified death.

Before I even entered the OR, I was inundated from those around me with a wide spectrum of moralistic directions to follow. These opinions were a blending of both the warzone and stateside moral codes. All I knew was that I had to appropriately treat this wounded American for not only would not doing so have morally destroyed me but also subjected him to a prolonged and horrible path to death; waiting for starvation, dehydration, sedation, depressed breathing, and decomposing devitalized tissue to weaken and poison him sufficiently to result in death.

During surgery I resected both hips with remaining lower legs, his sacrum and coccyx, and pubic and sitting bones, and there was still damage above that had to be addressed. To accomplish the goal of reaching undamaged tissue that would hopefully heal and not become infected, I used an amputation saw to cut across his lumbar (lower back) spine to effectively cut him in half.

His urinary tubes (ureters) and large intestine (sigmoid colon) were brought out to the skin so urine and stool could be evacuated.

A flap of buttock skin was preserved to swing up to cover the large defect (space) and enclose the abdominal contents. I placed a tracheostomy to ensure adequate breathing with a respirator to counter the increased pressure on the diaphragm from the intestinal overload in the reduced abdominal space. Then I amputated his irreparably damaged right hand and wrist.

The twenty-first century terminology for this operation is translumbar amputation. At the 85th Evac, the term was hemicorporectomy. In today's operating room six to ten specialists would convene to perform this surgery. Roger King and I were the only surgical participants.

He awoke and fully regained consciousness. He interacted and talked with the nurses, medics, and his constant screaming eagles buddies. I covered his remaining torso with sheets over a cradle.

One morning, as was the military routine, a brigadier general, his sergeant major, and other deferential kiss-ass brass swooped in to present purple hearts to the surviving wounded. I was observing the proceedings when I realized they were about to ignore my patient.

Clothed in a faded OD green T-shirt, my tie-dyed blue Bermuda shorts, and the ever-present love beads and broken peace sign, I stepped in the path of the general, saluted sloppily, pulled back the sheet covering the poor kid, and inquired if Richard Barbee were to receive any recognition. At the sight of half a man, the general became pale, staggered, regained some composure, and stuttered,

'Oh yes.' I got my point across without being court martialed.

He lived about two weeks and at the end died peacefully a day after things went south. Extraordinary measures were withheld to allow him to die with dignity."

Excerpted from my memoir; *Welcome Home From Vietnam, Finally,*
Chapter: *More Morbidity*

Visiting Richard Barbee at the Wall in Washington, DC

Here are more warriors whose names I never knew. **Their deaths are still in the forefront of my mind.**

"One late afternoon, on a sunny day, several of us were navigating a shortcut through the ED when the 85th Evac's base radio began to squawk. The receiver had picked up a clear transmission between an American patrol and its home firebase.

The sounds were loud, clear, and unmistakable. The radioman's voice echoed his terror.

This group of ten young American boys had stumbled into the midst of a NVA battalion in the Vietnam jungle.

They were woefully outnumbered and outgunned. The distinctive repetitive cracks of numerous AK47s firing were audible in the background as their young radioman was pleading for support and extraction. The terrified screams of the condemned Americans were palpable. The repetitive plaintive pleading from the radioman continued. Gradually, the volume of noise subsided until there was an empty haunting dead silence.

Twenty minutes later, a chopper landed on our helipad with all ten dead Americans. We checked them in the KIA shack for signs of life. There were none. In front of me lay the tanned and toned beautiful bodies that were still warm to touch. One had a crucifix around his neck. They were lying so peacefully with their heads gracefully tilted to the side they appeared to be asleep dreaming until one observed the lethal gaping bullet holes in their skulls, chests, and abdomens. One boy had lowered himself as much as possible against the ground, to avoid being hit, that the AK rounds had sliced across his back multiple times appearing as if he had been slashed with a knife.

This horribly distorted vile experience had attacked the integrity of my soul. I had witnessed the death of young Americans firsthand. They were not phantom references in a story. From a safe distance, I had shared the horror of imminent death with them. It was entirely different from engaging with a wounded stranger delivered to our ED doorstep. That day never leaves me."

Excerpted from my memoir *Welcome Home From Vietnam, Finally,*
Chapter: *Deadly Patrol*

The *Triage* function was morally and psychologically challenging.

"Our call sign was Plasma Hotel. As the medivac Huey approached, they would hide the M60 machine gun and send a transmission reflecting the number and seriousness of their precious cargo. The enemy used the Red Cross for target practice. No chopper was safe when within range of the enemy. The official interpretation of the Geneva Conventions was that the medivac Hueys could not be armed. Nonsense! They carried a M 60 machine gun that swung from bungee cords for protection, but once over friendly terrain, the weapon was detached.

The initial transmission was the number of KIA, i.e., killed in action. The dead were taken straight to and stacked, one on top of the other, in the KIA open-sided shack. One of Marilyn's first priorities as the new ED supervisor was to enclose the KIA shack. We, however, always checked for signs of life since a few were not actually dead and perhaps could be saved.

A gauge of the seriousness of the injuries aboard the Huey was reflected on how close the pilot landed to the ED doors.

Usually, the injured soldiers arrived in groups. Mass casualties involved many patients. Triage was performed to begin organizing efficient use of resources, personnel, operating rooms, blood, meds, etc.

KIAs needed no care.

Expectants were so damaged, so close to death, and required an inordinate amount of resources ultimately endangering the chances of survival of others. Therefore, they were placed behind a screen, given morphine, and allowed to die with dignity as a nurse held their hand and promised they would be OK. One expectant, I still recall, was a dying dehydrated, unintelligibly moaning boy whose skull on one side was missing and displayed slithering maggots nibbling on his devitalized brain tissue.

The *salvageable* were brought to the OR after resuscitation was initiated in the ED or laterally evacuated to other hospitals, as the 95th Evac in Da Nang, which had medical specialists we did not.

The *last triage group* were those whose injuries did not require immediate definitive care. They were operated upon when the OR's cleared of current patients with life-threatening injuries."

Excerpted from my memoir, *Welcome Home From Vietnam, Finally,*
Chapter: *Medivac*

Let's change the mood. This unknown grunt's wounding had a happy ending.

"Now traveling to the other side of the emotional scale, let's consider another of my experiences.

Two drunken grunts were acting out in their hooch. Loaded weapons were ubiquitous. In a morbid jest, one kid picked up his 38 revolver, and in pretending to shoot his buddy actually did. The victim arrived in the ED via ambulance in stable condition.

The usual procedures were instituted (you should be well versed by now), and he was brought to the OR. The routine abdominal x-ray had been taken to see where the bullet was located. On inspection of the film, it resided in the upper abdomen but was accompanied by another metallic object. He had been shot once! There was only one bullet hole.

At surgery, various organs were repaired, and the bleeding stopped. A distorted fully jacketed 38 slug was retrieved along with a caved in St. Christopher's Medal. Long considered the patron saint of travelers, he was un-sainted in 1969. But if one wishes, they might accept that the saint, through this medal as it resided over the boy's heart, performed a miracle. The potentially lethal bullet had struck the medal and deflected it into his abdomen instead of penetrating his heart.

Whoever or whatever was responsible, it was a miracle!"

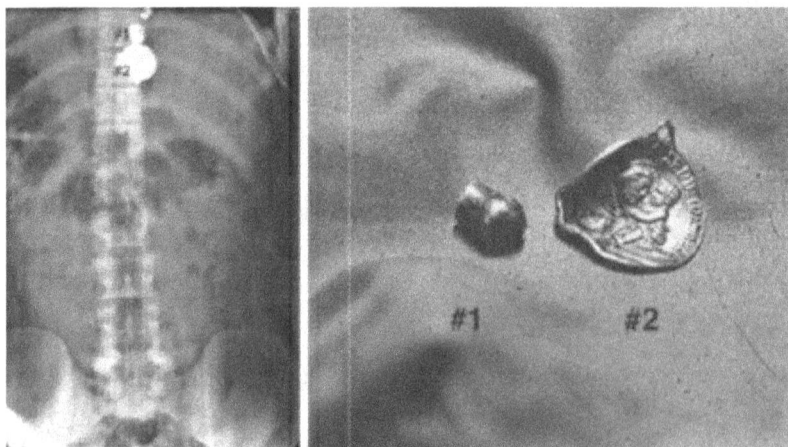

The bullet and medal from the Saint Christopher miracle

Excerpt from my memoir, *Welcome Home From Vietnam, Finally,*
Chapter: *More Morbidity.*

1 August 1971

1 AUG 71

Hi / Helen + Jim

Got your doctor's note —
I'm not much to say but
I don't know him — but
tell if he does good + if
you like him so do I —
Don't go around distrusting
everyone RIGHT —— RIGHT!

— Same old shit —
I'm finally getting
short — got some new
Sergeant's today. Sm
[illegible] a little more
[illegible] maybe again

Better read the notice

Jno
Eddie

Complete Letter

1 AUG 71

Hi Helene + Jim

Got your doctor's note - I've not much to say - I don't know him - but hell if he has a good rep + you like him go ahead - can't go around distrusting everyone - Right - Right!

Same old shit -

I'm finally getting short - got some new surgeons today. Can play around a little more now - might be Japan

Better read the notice

Love
Eddie

An Explanation

I know you have been confused by the signing of my Vietnam letters with *Eddie* .

Here's the deal. My sister, Helene, knew me as **Eddie.**

Prior to their wedding, my mother negotiated several ground rules with my father.

I would be named, as his parents insisted, Gustav Edward Kappler III.

She disliked the name Gus and referred to my father as Kappy. Their compromise was that I would be christened with the full family name but referred to as Eddie.

That lasted until I entered Cornell University when I became *Gus.*

Retrospective

That was my last advice to Helene concerning her abnormal pap smear.

"Same old shit" I felt that enough was enough!

During the last month and a half of my stay at the 85th Evac., the volume of casualties diminished markedly. I had too much down time. That lack of responsibility and being "short" were a dangerous combination.

I was presented with an inclusive notice to be sent home warning those who would interact with us of what abnormal speech and actions that may occur. Just a small portion is shown but you'll get the idea.

NOTICE OF RETURN TO THE UNITED STATES

Issued in solemn warning this 7th day of August 19 __ : To the friends, relatives, neighbors, and acquaintances of Gus Kappler MD MC

Very soon the above named person will once again be in your midst; dehydrated, demoralized, and de-Americanized, but once again he will be ready to take his place as a human being, engaged in life, liberty, and a somewhat belated pursuit of happiness.

In making your joyous preparations to welcome him back into respectable society, you must make allowances for the very crude environment which has been his home for the last months. In a word, he may be somewhat Asiaticized and suffering from Viet Cong-itis or perhaps too much Ba Mui Ba.

Show no alarm if he prefers to squat rather than sit on a chair. Keep cool if he prefers to wear silk pajamas and carry a basket of rice, old bread and chopsticks. He may run around in sandals and a towel, slyly offering to sell cigarettes to the postman, and pick suspiciously at his food as though he thought you were trying to poison him. Above all, ask permission before mentioning such food delicacies of the Far East, such as "Flied Lice" (fried rice).

Most of those I was closest to had gone back to the "world." The remainder were equally bored. I had no connection with the newbie surgeons; they did not yet understand our mind set. Recording the reel-to-reel tapes was complete, we were photographically wasted, and

I was hoping for a medical accompaniment with recovering patients to Japan for relief.

I decided that the fewer daylight hours I endured in Vietnam the faster I'd depart from this nightmare. A number of us began to party, play cards, throw dice, and commiserate into the wee hours of the morning. This activity was followed by seeking an induced sleep in my uncomfortable metal cot under the entombing mosquito netting. I'd then arise at twelve noon or one o'clock to begin the next day. This activity certainly was destructive; *self-medicate with alcohol and using sleep to bury our existence. I was experiencing a downward spiral culminating in disaster five days before the day I was due to DEROS (officially go home).*

"Bob was about to leave Vietnam and the 85th Evac. I had about five days remaining.

Casey MCed the obligatory Hi-Bye Party in the club. I regaled Bob on stage with my usual sixth grade level poetry. We all celebrated having become brothers in this vile-disgusting place.

I arranged for a party to end all parties for the next night. Docs, officers, medics, pilots, nurses, and enlisted were all welcome. The BBQ pit that we built was fired up early. The mountain of steaks was marinated. Gallons of beer were chilled.

Our world was good.

I spent the entire afternoon in Marylin's hooch (she was the ED nurse supervisor married to a chopper pilot) helping her make a mega quantity of Philippine egg rolls. That's the intelligent decision. The stupid action was the entire time producing egg rolls, I serially devoured chunks of fruit that were soaking in absolute alcohol I had procured from the pathology lab. All this on an empty stomach.

By party time I was close to anesthetic, but I did assume my responsibility of cooking the egg rolls in our electric frying pan using the wall of a nearby hooch for support. Obviously, I had more to drink.

Gus frying Philippine egg rolls

We had procured a fuel bladder and transitioned it into an above the ground pool after cleaning the inside and filling it with water.

It was close to 2:00 a.m. when I decided, having been a lifeguard, that we all were too incapacitated to continue jumping the five feet from the nearby bunker into the 'pool.'

I announced such from on top of the bunker. I noticed a blurred splash of someone disobeying my directive. I jumped in the direction of the 'pool.' I missed, not by a lot but enough to land with my feet on a metal-folding chair and with my right arm attempting to balance myself by reaching for the side of the fuel bladder.

All this resulted in a fracture dislocation of my right elbow. I remember sitting on the ground initially not being able to move my fingers. There were enough functioning synapses in my brain for me to consider that this stupid drunken act may have ended my surgical career. Much to my relief, finger movement returned within the hour.

Without an orthopedic surgeon, we reduced my elbow as some of Casey's happy juice floated in my veins. A cast was applied by someone to my right arm from mid-upper arm to my wrist. Right!

I could not bend my arm and became a clumsy lefty. I was told to sleep everything off in the ICU, but after a few hours, I went back to my hooch to begin packing for my evacuation home. It took three to four hours to organize, pack cardboard boxes, and tape them securely.

I kept my washed-out fatigues on. I figured the major's insignia would buffer me a bit from the army bullshit I was about to encounter. I could not lace up my boots, so I chose non-army issue loafers and wore them all the way home.

Just before I was to climb into the jeep for my ride to the Phu Bai Airport, a group of nurses presented me with a large tray of weed enhanced brownies to help mellow me during my travels. Truthfully, I do not remember but a few hours of my flight from Japan to our Alaskan stop. I wonder if my dosage of that chemical gave me retrograde amnesia.

I was flown from Phu Bai to Saigon, stayed a night, was flown to Japan, stayed a night, then left for home.

After Bob had arrived home, he called Robin and gave her the facts. His information was quite helpful because she and my parents had received that yellow telegram. Its message was that I had disconnected my right arm while diving into the officer's club swimming pool.

She also called a colonel in Washington DC for clarification, and his reply was that 'this is the funniest thing to come in all week.'

I called Robin from Japan. The transmission was so clear I felt she was around the corner. I told her I'd be fine and would see her soon. It was a ninety-dollar call but worth it."

Excerpted from my memoir, *Welcome Home From Vietnam, Finally,*
Chapter: *Inauspicious Departure.*

Epilogue

Upon my arrival home, Robin had planned to meet me at the airport with her hugs and Kim and Chris waving American flags. That was until my inauspicious departure from Vietnam.

She did call her medical contact in Washington and learned that I would be evacuated to Valley Forge Army Hospital. Leaving the children at home, she drove six hours alone to Pennsylvania worrying about me.

"So, there I was in the skies over the Pacific totally relaxed eating my juiced brownies. I do not remember landing in Japan but there was a Boy Scout World Jamboree taking place on that island country. An American boy scout's asthma became exacerbated, and he was given a ride home in our C-141. I'm not sure when but I was shaken awake by an Air Force flight nurse who advised me I needed to treat the boy scout for he was having problems. I have no idea what I utilized to treat him, but they did not bother me again. I awoke as we were about to land in Alaska. We deplaned, celebrated being on American soil, bought junk food, and selected Alaskan dolls for our children.

The C-141 next landed at an airport near the army post of Ft. Dix, New Jersey. We were transported to a nearby facility to stay overnight. A bus delivered a group of us to Valley Forge General Hospital where Robin was awaiting my arrival. She had planned the stereotypical welcome home.

I still had the same washed-out fatigues. I was sitting near admissions with the other patients when I spotted Robin heading to the window to ask where I was.

I stood and she came over, and we greeted in a reserved manner.

Well, they soon dressed me in the standard blue Army hospital PJs, and I became one of hundreds wandering the halls. I was placed in a single room. Robin came with me, and as she was sitting at my bedside, a bossy nurse poked her head in and shouted, 'Don't close the door.' Sure, I wanted to be with Robin, but in a bustling hospital?

My right arm was elevated with my elbow at a right angle. I was given physical therapy to increase the range of motion of my elbow. I was amazed at how difficult it was to regain adequate function. I called **Ed Kayser** , an orthopedist (my medical school roommate), and he advised me not to let Valley Forge's orthopedists surgically remove my radial head. They did suggest that procedure, and I refused. After bombarding me with multiple reasons why I would regret my decision, they finally left me alone.

My resulting disability was the inability to fully extend and flex my arm at the elbow by a few degrees. Thankfully, there was no impairment of my surgical skills. None of the previously predicted complications developed. But I could forget golf and tennis. I tried southpaw, but it did not work out.

My first official visitor at Valley Forge was a full bird colonel Army Catholic chaplain who, without requiring me to say a word, waved his hand over me making the sign of the cross absolving me of all wayward activity in Vietnam. I guess the typical soldier's laundry list of offenses was too long and repetitive to listen to over and over again.

I felt a sense of deprecation from the hospital physicians and nurses. Robin suggested, and I agreed to wear my khakis with my major designation when in the hospital. What a difference a little golden leaf made.

Word of my arrival spread rapidly. A number of 85th Evac nurses and the patients I had operated on visited me. I easily recognized the nurses. The soldiers were another matter, for they had gained weight, grown their hair long, and sprouted facial hair. To identify the patients, I would ask them to lift up their shirt so that I could see their unique abdominal incisions, drain sites, and various other holes."

Excerpted from my memoir, *Welcome Home From Vietnam, Finally,*
Chapter: *Inauspicious Departure*

Contradictory to my written orders to be stationed at Ft. Carson, Colorado, the commander at Valley Forge maneuvered to keep me there for the remainder of my active-duty commitment. I successfully resisted.

I enjoyed a month's medical leave at Lake Panamoka on Long Island, NY in the house Robin had rented near her father. My family then set off for Colorado Springs, Colorado. We drove across the country to Ft. Carson. I was amazed that the United States was essentially flat from Rochester, NY to the Rockies. I was relieved to discover the lack of humidity once we left New York State.

In the Prologue you have read about my state of mind, and depth of PTSD when back in the United States. Robin's verbal intervention to immediately address my polluted mind-set was the game changer.

"Most of the docs at Ft. Carson's hospital had been in Vietnam. This post was a choice assignment and preference was given to those who had been in that combat zone. Our social life developed around our physician specialty groupings and former Vietnam friends. Excessive drinking and a fair amount of cannabis consumption were the norm for doctors newly returning from Vietnam. Robin and I hosted a party soon after arriving in Colorado. After everyone had returned home, hearing my voice, she searched the house for me. I could not be found until she entered the backyard to find me sitting on a tree limb, about fifteen feet up, screaming at the 'F——ing Vietnamese.' I had toxic levels of alcohol and Cannabis in my system.

The beauty of being with men who had the same experiences was that we were safe to express our feelings, nightmares, self- doubts, regrets, and cries for help in a receptive understanding environment.

As time progressed, we learned to not depend on pot and drinking as an avenue of escape, but to begin to cope with our issues, to (consciously *not* unconsciously *as in Vietnam)* compartmentalize wartime traumatic events, and to begin to focus on our potentially fulfilling futures, leaving the past in the past."

Excerpted from my memoir, *Welcome Home From Vietnam, Finally,*
Chapter: *Ft. Carson, Colorado*

Without stigmatization, while living and interacting with the other doctors at Ft. Carson, who had also served in Vietnam, I began to understand my predicament. In ***trusting and sharing*** with these Veterans, the stigma of PTSD was removed. I discovered ***my descent into PTSD was predictable*** as reflected in the commonality of our traumatic experiences. We were now better equipped to face our threatening demons.

Remember!

You are *not alone.* You

are **not** *unique.* You are

not weak.

As I, *you did not have a chance!*

The key for rehabilitation is to *seek out others and share your stories.*

Vietnam Veterans, seek out an *Honor Flight* to be welcomed home. In the Albany, NY and Manhattan, NY areas contact: **Greg Furlong** at gfurlong9296@gmail.com .

Vietnam and Post 911 Veterans, first responders, police, firefighters, others with PTSD related to their profession should contact: **Bob Nevins** at *Alliance180.org* .

Different Initial Pathways

Prior to Vietnam, my time at Ft. Sam Houston in basic training masqueraded as the real thing. The topic of high velocity wounding that we would treat in Vietnam from semi auto rifles, booby traps, and other ordinance was never discussed. Never was the subject of high-velocity wounding introduced.

My advantage was in having completed my rigorous surgical training at the Medical College of Virginia in Richmond, VA under Dr. David Hume. Roger King and I easily switched gears to surgically approach the devastation of battlefield wounds. We were experienced and confident in our judgement.

"The first AK-47 GSW (high velocity) of the thorax that I attended, a thru and thru of the upper right chest, was initially treated by me with a a chest drainage system worked state side for most GSW's (low velocity).

Tracy, an ICU nurse, called me to say 'Gus, there's a lot of blood and air coming out of the chest tube.' We were all on a first basis for all were equally important in-patient care. There was no rank involved in our relationships; just respect for a 100% effort.

After returning to my hooch to review the right lung's anatomy, I took the grunt to the OR and removed the hemorrhaging and pulverized upper portion of his lung."

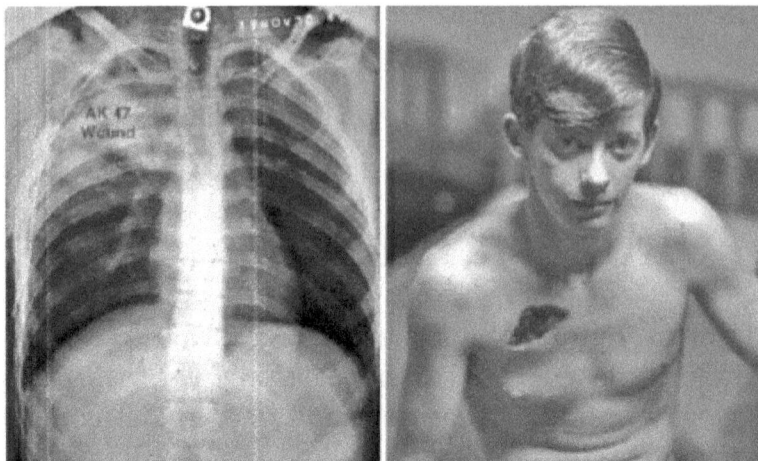

In the preoperative chest x-ray, the damaged lung is white.
Photo of the eighteen-year-old kid postoperatively with an open wound.

Since we considered our OR environment a petri dish
of bacteria, to avoid infection we never primarily
sutured the skin and underlying fat to avoid
infection. Wounds were sutured closed after five to
seven days - Delayed Primary Closure or DPC.

From *Welcome Home From Vietnam, Finally,* Chapter: *Nurses*

We did crawl under low wires with machine guns firing overhead and fake explosions. However, the basic's most dangerous episode occurred when those not familiar with guns turned in threatening directions waving loaded weapons with the gun safety on off.

The most fun part was completing the night compass course as beer infused doctors. We bribed a medic to deliver a cold case of beer to us at the starting point. We dutifully learned that two cans of beer fit nicely into our web belt's canteen cup - sans the canteen.

We were **not stripped** of who we were and through stigmatization, remodeled into killing machines.

Stigmatize

Oxford Thesaurus of English, 2nd edition

To mark with stigmata by

condemning, denouncing, branding, defaming, or labeling

Listen to a veteran confirm the transition: **Military Abandonment:**
https://youtu.be/_jPjsyFr1SI?si=1bBm_niwtuhbrH1O

The warriors to be, primarily with adolescent mental function, were torn away from the *morality of peace* with killing prohibited and forced to function under the *morality of war.* That is, killing mechanically at a moment's notice reacting to a perceived enemy or when ordered.

Warriors suffer a moral injury when existing in a *moral limbo* vacillating between both moral codes - *never exclusively* in either one. Every veteran I've interviewed, especially those who were snipers, admitted that after killing an enemy combatant, they felt a trace of guilt from their moral code of peace - their lifelong experience until entering the military.

Those of us not exposed to legitimate basic training

remained influenced by the moral code of peace - killing prohibited. We obviously understood that killing was the object of combat, but we were never trained that killing was our objective. We were physicians, surgeons, and nurses sent to Vietnam as totally naive military personnel to heal the sick and wounded.

We had not the slightest idea of what we would encounter in a combat zone. For me, those wartime experiences would be indelibly traumatizing. We had read about and watched war movies that spoke of WWI "shell shock" and WWII "battle fatigue" but had no reason to research those mental aberrations. Little did I know that I would be polluted during my year in Vietnam with what we labeled "Delayed Stress." In 1980 it was defined officially as Post Traumatic Stress Disorder - PTSD.

Having not been exposed to legitimate military basic training and indoctrination, the 85th Evac. medical personnel brains *subconsciously* **compartmentalized - buried -** their traumatic experiences. The consequences of which are delineated in my descent into anger and pain.

Those conditioned to kill, the grunts, exist in a *'moral limbo'* that I earlier described. However, they are ruled by *'stigmatization'* and are forced to live up to imposed standards of conduct. **Since they do not share their feelings, they perceive themselves to be alone, to be unique in their suffering, and consider themselves weak when they experience suffering after having killed another human being. They do not have a chance to avoid PTSD.**

The mechanism that creates great warriors is through *stigmatization.* That is to stigmatize repeatedly in front of one's peers and superiors and force the adolescent warrior into accepting the military culture of killing as a duty. Control of the military unit is then established, as each warrior is reshaped by utilizing stigmatization.

As championed by Lt. Col.(R) David Grossman, in *On Combat,* the goal is to maintain the brain of each warrior close to the *"fight or flight" response.* He referred to that circumstance as *The Beast.* That state of mind is the goal in combat, but it also *goes into overdrive when a warrior is feeling alone, feeling unique, and feeling weak, helpless, and depressed.*

Without relief of the increased *"fight or flight"* within the adolescent warrior's brains, there is destruction of brain cells and a delay in expected brain maturation, and the inducement of substance abuse.

The weed, alcohol, and heroin sought by the warrior to relieve their symptoms cause additional brain damage and symptomatology. The vicious circle of momentary relief followed by increased symptomatology resulting in continued substance abuse leads to a *brain disharmony* wherein suicide becomes the most "rational" next step for relief.

Without exception, from Vietnam to the Post 911 wars and conflicts, the active warrior is abruptly discharged or reassigned into a *"sink or swim"* environment.

Psychological testing may be given but the soldier still on active duty *remains in the stigmatized mode.* They will not admit their true feelings. They also want to get home as quickly as possible. Those remaining in the military are fearful of jeopardizing their advancement.

The military employs *ineffective attempts* to counsel an emerging veteran in his rehabilitation and reintegration into a peaceful society. Many veterans struggle when out from under the "military's wing" of essentially total support. Some warriors become addicted to the "fight or flight" mentality and are unable to function in a peaceful society. These altered individuals often re-enter active duty to satisfy their absence of heightened activity that accompanies combat.

Tragically, the discharged warrior lacks support when floundering at home. Why?

The Veterans Administration continues to flub their perceived efforts to address damaged veterans.

Pursue the following links for exposure of the VA's failures.

A new Government Accountability Office report says that the Department of Defense isn't verifying if at-risk troops actually get the help they need reentering civilian life. *Task&Purpose:* https://taskandpurpose.com/military-life/departmant-of-defense- troops-veterans-reentering-civilian-life-transition-program/

Discover the damaged federal hotline: "the national hotline for veterans suffering a mental health crisis was struggling to keep its responders trained" and " 'It's certainly not a best practice to be trying to assess two people at the same time for suicide,' a former Crisis Line worker told *Task&Purpose.* " https://taskandpurpose.com/ military-life/gao-report-veteran-crisis-line-procedures/?

"Almost 90% of service members interviewed for the RAND report indicated they would limit what they share with mental health providers because of privacy concerns." *Task&Purpose* article: https:// taskandpurpose.com/news/mental-health-privacy-rand-report/

"Veteran advocates are asking for accountability on how the Department of Veterans Affairs uses its $571 million suicide prevention budget, and whether those efforts are working."

To learn about the VA's continuing ineffectiveness please read another *Task&Purpose* article:https:// taskandpurpose.com/news/ veteran-suicide-prevention-accountability/

"Two-thirds of troops who left the military in 2023 were at risk for mental health conditions, survey found" *Task&Purpose* article: https:// taskandpurpose.com/ military-life/gao-report-mental-health-screening/

As previously discussed, self-medicating results in a vicious cycle destroying the brain's harmony. This state of disharmony inhibits the brain's normal function and suicide becomes the most reasonable alternative in combating a warrior's demons and helplessness.

This disharmony and the risk of suicide are explored in detail by me in: *Confronting Military PTSD and Suicide:* https://youtu.be/ ajT9-LOF6R8?si=3df-jI9KA9De6DtN

Without exception, from Vietnam to the Post 911 wars and conflicts, the active warrior is abruptly discharged or reassigned to emotionally *"sink or swim."* Psychological testing may be given by the military but the soldier still on active duty *remains in the stigmatized mode.* They will not admit their true feelings. They also want to get home as quickly as possible. Those remaining in the service are fearful of jeopardizing advancement.

The military employs *ineffective attempts* to counsel an emerging veteran in his rehabilitation and reintegration into a peaceful society. Many veterans struggle when out from under the "military's wing" of essentially total support. Some warriors become addicted to the "fight or flight" mentality and are unable to function in a peaceful society. These altered individuals often re-enter active duty to satisfy their absence of organization or heightened activity that accompanies combat.

The **Prevention of PTSD** must become the goal of our military. Pie in the sky? Not at all!

Gilbert J. Brown PhD., Professor Emeritus in Department of Health Care Policy, stated in *Unleashing the Power of Prevention (2015) that currently we treat psychological problems after they are identified.* **Behavioral health problems can be prevented.** *Prevention is the best investment we can make, and the time to make it is now before behavioral problems cascade."*

The US Air Force will, before discharge, arrange for their airmen and women to participate in the **Deployment Transition Center (DTC).** Located in Ramstein, Germany, outside of the war zone in a stress free and safe environment, the subjects are encouraged to rest, relax, defuse, and decompress with similarly affected airmen and women. The object is for them to learn that they share the same traumatic experiences and that **they are not alone in feeling weak, helpless, unique, and depressed.**

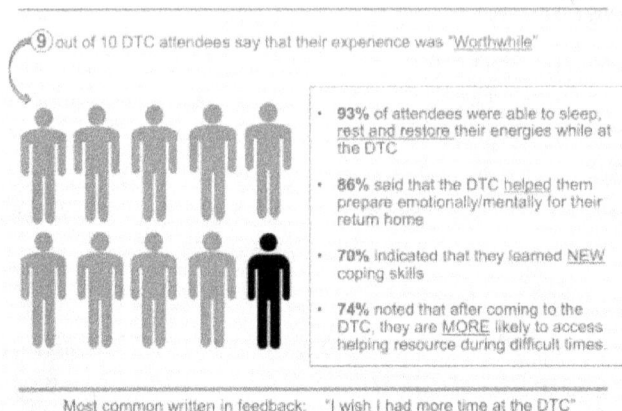

9 out of 10 DTC attendees say that their experience was "Worthwhile"

- **93%** of attendees were able to sleep, rest and restore their energies while at the DTC

- **86%** said that the DTC helped them prepare emotionally/mentally for their return home

- **70%** indicated that they learned NEW coping skills

- **74%** noted that after coming to the DTC, they are MORE likely to access helping resource during difficult times.

Most common written in feedback: "I wish I had more time at the DTC"

Deployment Transition Center's admirable results

Brig. General Mordente, USAF, commented "There are wounds that our (service members) carry you can't see. What I'm proud to say, is because of the DTC, *we do have an answer.* "

The warrior's **superiors** are not in attendance.

There is **no record keeping.** *The threat to stigmatization is therefore eliminated.*

This Air Force effort has resulted in a *forty percent decrease in PTSD symptoms* after discharge associated with significant improvement in alcohol consumption, conflicts, and sleep disturbance.

PTSD may occur in the Israel Defense Force (IDF), but in a minority of warriors. All their citizens, except for one minority group, are compelled to serve actively and in the reserves.

By default, because of the density of active duty and veteran warriors, the symptoms of descent into **PTSD** have become common knowledge. Their military is proactive. Being symptomatic is *not stigmatized*. Setting the precedent, the more senior military leaders are transparent concerning their seeking psychological support.

The **Air Force DTC** mirrors *my Plea* for the military to employ a *preventive strategy* . I call this approach a *Therapeutic Time Out* offered *PRIOR* to discharge. It would be the *DTC on steroids* which would process *all soon to be veterans with their unit* .

As recommended by Col. Eyal Fruchter (R), when Chief of Israeli Armed Forces Mental Health, "to prevent PTSD the proposed program should take advantage of the cohesiveness and supportive strength of the *warrior's existing unit* ."

The objective would be teaching them the basics of post military survival. Also of critical importance, to reinforce that *they are not alone in feeling weak, unique, and helpless - that sharing is imperative for understanding and dealing with their new state of mind.*

Here is my YouTube video pleading for the Pentagon to adopt a routine **Therapeutic Time Out Prior to Discharge:** *Plea to our Military:* https://youtu.be/T9EMz23LBZk?si=ym2_Rs_8YGVgRkC7

Remember that -

You are *not alone.*

You are **not** *unique.*

You are *not weak.*
As I, *you did not have a chance!*

The key for rehabilitation is to *seek
out others and share your stories.*

Jeff Schogol's August 15, 2025, Task&Purpose Article Says it

All Here are pertinent excerpts from veteran quotes

"...veterans must acknowledge that they have an invisible injury..."

"It's something you really can't lock away from. Any veteran that tries to do that is making a real mistake."

"Drugs and alcohol may provide temporary relief, but numbing is not the answer. They won't fix anything."

"...veterans get through tough times by talking to each other."

"I had to share experiences with guys I'd served with, with somebody who was interested... try to explain feelings and try to explain how it has kind of affected me."

Sound familiar?

"Gus is still angry"

Yes, that is the title of my **ECHOES** interview by the Vietnam Veterans Memorial Fund. https://echoes-of-the-vietnam-war.simplecast.com/ episodes/gus-kappler

Why? There are two major contributors.

First, the *fallacy* of our military's involvement in Vietnam and the senseless sacrifice of our youth's minds, bodies, and souls.

Second, the *war crime* of indiscriminately spraying the defoliant/ herbicide Agent Orange, containing a vicious Dioxin, over a sovereign country and consequently poisoning not only our warriors but generations of Vietnamese. Both populations are threatened with devastating illness and birth defects in the newborn.

There are sites in Vietnam where the poison was stored which to this day test strongly positive for Dioxin.

This evil mutagenic and carcinogenic chemical leaches into the groundwater and it is absorbed by the algae small fish eat. These bait fish are eaten by larger fish that are harvested for consumption by the Vietnamese population.

The *fallacy* was addressed in the retrospectives of my letters to Helene. Now it's time to discuss the *war crime.*

The term **Agent Orange** encompasses a rainbow of defoliant/ herbicide combinations sprayed over South Vietnam, i.e., Blue, White, Green, Pink, Purple, and Orange. Most colors contained

2,4,5-T contaminated with Dioxin. Blue contained arsenic which does not degrade and poisons forever.

Record keeping was faulty, but most will agree that due to the Operation Ranch Hand program, approximately 20,000,000 gallons of defoliant/herbicidal poison were sprayed between 1960 and 1972 over South Vietnam.

Please see: https://en.wikipedia.org/wiki/Agent_Orange

Presidents Kennedy, Johnson , and Nixon were fully aware of the "Rainbow's" toxicity and condoned its usage while mindlessly sacrificing those serving in Vietnam and poisoning the Vietnamese people.

In fact, the **United Nations** accused the United States of violating the Geneva Protocols limiting chemical and biological weapons. The United States vetoed any official action.

That's a *war crime*.

The rationale of spraying was to defoliate Vietnam's jungle vegetation to reveal the enemy; to destroy the rice crops thus preventing the VC and NVA from successfully foraging for food; and to drive citizens into the cities. All the goals were to some extent accomplished.

Agent Orange is a 50/50 mixture of 2,4-D and 2,4,5-T. The first chemical is readily available at Home Depot or Lowes.

The *criminality* is defined by ignoring the fact that in the manufacture of 2,4,,5-T an extremely toxic chemical, **a *Dioxin*,** was a *predictable* by-product in its manufacture. A drop of this dioxin in four million gallons of water caused cancer in laboratory rats; *one thousand times* *that* concentration was sprayed over our troops and most of South Vietnam. Former Vietnam grunts will confirm the "sticky liquid" falling on them while on patrol in the jungle.

In response to my online discussion concerning Agent Orange, Vietnam veterans Bernard Downey, Larry Wright, and Richard Miller informed me that the poison was stored next to the 85th Evacuation Hospital while I served there.

Richard Miller stated: "I was beside that Hospital (85th Evac.) In 1970/1971. 1 helped load AO on spray adapted aircraft right there, some barrels had rusted leaking bottoms, I had it running down my arms and all over my hands, no one told us to wear gloves."

Bernard stated: "What genius thought it was a good idea to store AO next to the hospital?!!"

The suppliers, Monsanto and Dow Chemical, were fully aware of Agent Orange's toxicity. The military scientists were fully aware.

However, as reported in Admiral E.R. Zumwalt's May 5, 1990 *Report to the Secretary of the Department of Veteran Affairs,* naive and sheltered men of science green lighted the use of Agent Orange. They truly believed that *it would only be sprayed on the enemy.* They also added that if accidentally our troops were poisoned, *our country would care for them* . Unbelievable!

The 1990 report also documented the VA's deliberate manipulation of data to disprove the herbicides' culpability as follows:

 "Unfortunately, **political interference** in government sponsored studies associated with Agent Orange has been the norm, not the exception. In fact, there appears to have been a *systematic effort* to suppress critical data or alter results to meet preconceived notions of what alleged scientific studies were meant to find."

"....there appeared to be a **purposeful effort to sabotage** any chance of a meaningful Agent Orange exposure analysis."

and

"......strongly hints at a **discernible pattern**, *if not outright governmental collaboration,* to deny compensation to Vietnam Veterans for disabilities associated with exposure to dioxin."

Executives at Dow Chemical published reports refuting their herbicide's toxicity: https://www.sourcewatch.org/index. php?title=Paul_F_Oreffice&oldid=699804

Is my anger a reasonable reaction?

It took twenty years of constant pressure for the Veterans Administration to recognize the "Rainbow's" induced veteran disabilities. New illnesses have recently been added to the long list. As we Vietnam veterans lament, **"Agent Orange is the gift that keeps on giving."**

To learn the current list of disabilities, please visit: https:// www. publichealth.va.gov/exposures/agentorange/conditions/ index.asp

All this hits home, for up to this date, eighteen of our 85th Evacuation Hospital beloved personnel have developed Agent Orange derived illnesses resulting in eight deaths. These sacrificed healers were part of my family for a year. Their demise - unnecessary, disturbing, and heart breaking.

85th Evacuation Hospital Agent Orange Victims

I have suffered colon cancer (denied by the VA), multiple skin basal cell cancers, melanoma of the face, Chronic Lymphocytic Leukemia, and atrial fibrillation with heart failure.

Were we at the 85h Evac. exposed to Agent Orange? Most definitely!

54,000 gallons of actual Agent Orange was sprayed by C-123 planes over the Phu Bai area where the 85th Evac. was built. The amounts of this defoliant/herbicide sprayed by hand and helicopter were not recorded. There is no information related to the other rainbow herbicides.

Please visit this site for amounts sprayed over various South Vietnam localities : https://cybersarges.tripod.com/AOphotos.html

We inhaled the contaminated dust, drank the contaminated water, and encountered the contamination on the fatigues of the wounded. We had no idea we were being poisoned as the reward for serving our country as the dedicated healers of young sick and wounded Americans.

C-123 plane adapted for the spraying of Agent Orange

All who served in Vietnam, the land veterans and those on adjacent waters never had a chance. We developed illnesses and our children and grandchildren were at risk.

Angry, hell yes over the past.

But, even more so when considering the same indifferent approach to the **Post 911 veteran illnesses** which were triggered due to being blanketed in toxic fumes emanating from **burn pits** adjacent to their combat zone living quarters.

Again, it took almost twenty years for the Veterans Administration to admit the pentagon's culpability and award disability designations.

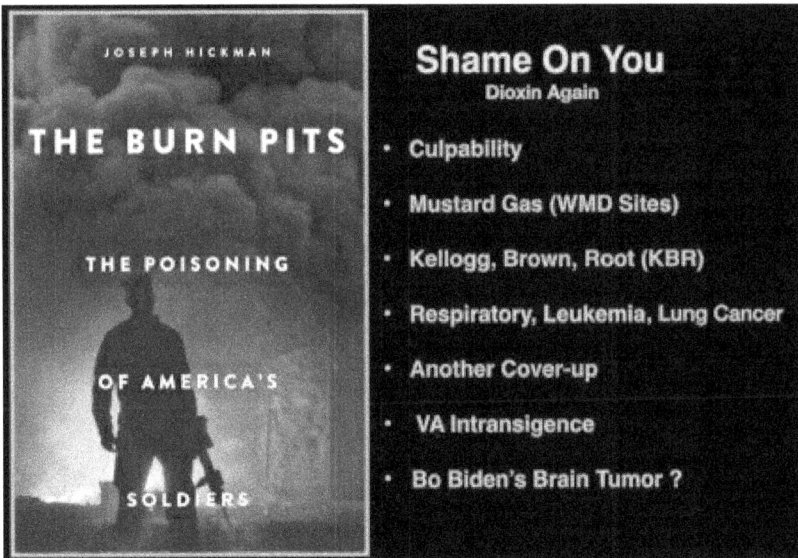

THE BURN PITS, the poisoning of America's Soldiers

Last Thoughts

To those who govern us:

Will elected officials ever read and abide by previously recorded failures, consider our warriors as equally human, and accept the fact that they must be returned home "whole?"

Shockingly. politicians continue to condone and perpetuate the attitudes of the humanity deficient General Patton. Our brave men and women continue to be discharged to *"sink or swim."*

I realize warriors die in combat but please do not treat them as totally expendable.

I just received a sad email from **Wes**, a dear friend from my year at the 85th Evacuation Hospital.

He relates a tragic example of our government's abandoning post 911 warriors to "sink or swim."

"We also are deeply affected by PTSD. Our son Pete passed away in December awaiting a liver transplant. The self-medicating with alcohol to control the demons and ravages of PTSD from one tour in Afghanistan and two tours in Iraq with the 10th Mountain division finally took their toll. We had his funeral with military honors at Bay Pines National Cemetery in January and many of his friends from the Army were there coming from all around the country. It was very moving and has helped us to cope with his loss. The reunion* is just around the corner. **It will be good to see everyone**"

Excerpts from a recent email I received from Marilyn H.

Marilyn was career military RN and the director of the 85th Evac.'s ED. She and I made the Philippine egg rolls that lead to my right elbow's demise. Page 114.

Robert, her second husband, was a company commander fighting the NVA in I Corps. We have attended many 85th Evac. reunions together.

She said:

"I suffered with PTSD all of my time in the military *after* Vietnam. I countered it by working 12-16 *hours* per duty day."

"*I did not give myself time* to think about the horrors we all went through that 1 year in the midst of war. When I got home I was so tired to do anything but take a shower and go to bed."

"At work, I had OCD, *very strict and demanded perfection.*"

"Everything about PTSD *changed when I retired.* I cried the entire time I was getting my discharge physical. I cried and became hysterical when I was diagnosed with Breast Cancer during my discharge physical."

"Many hours attending counseling sessions and groups… *None of the sessions helped …*"

"I found another job which again kept me in the *same schedule as when I was active duty.*"

"Now Robert and I are fully retired from everything. We both have PTSD, his is more severe. *We try to live with the bad dreams* and often argue about nothing, keep our many frequent medical appts of every part of our To be inserted anatomies, and continue to have *problems making friends within the civilian community.*"

Excerpts from an email I received from Duane W. on August 30, 2025

"I am still sad that we cannot connect next month*. To use the words of a famous surgeon from the 85th Evac., 'Our reunions are those of a family still looking for answers and redemptions.'"

"*I found some solace* last year when we had a casual visit with others in the common room. Without you, those connections have less value, some of *'the family'* will not be there. *The journey for answers and redemption continues....*"

"I was anxious to introduce you to Kathryn, the new lady in my life. I am very blessed that someone has *accepted this soul with baggage who continues to look for answers and redemption*

Your comrade in scrubs....QUESTION MAN**"

Question Man - Duane W., Army ED and OR medic at the 85th Evac.

After fifty-five years, all who attend our 85th Evac. reunions do so to continue with their healing from persistent "demons and ravages."

Utilizing the information I presented in Letters, why don't you form a group to analyze both massages concentrating on the italicized segments?

* The 85th Evac. 2025 Reunion in Las Vegas that I could not attend.

** As an inquisitive twenty-year-old Army medic, he overwhelmed me with his questions. Therefore, I arranged for his scrub shirts to be adorned with a huge question mark. Duane was required to wear the garment at the hospital.

To the reader:

I've always believed that recording and studying history is of paramount educational importance.

For over half a century I have done so. All the information in *Letters*
is factual.

I hope the reader has been enlightened concerning the evolution of PTSD, that *we are all susceptible,* and that PTSD may be dealt with by prevention or retroactive engagement.

Gus has *"Been there , done that."*

I'm eighty-six years old and still angry about the injustice I received from my country. However, **I emphatically** do not regret my service as a thirty-year-old Army trauma surgeon, I saved a lot of kids.

I do regret what it cost me emotionally. I also regret the necessity of experiencing the weighty requirement of learning how to re-engage living in a peaceful society. I also wish I had not been poisoned by Agent Orange.

However, that episode of my life spent in a Vietnam combat zone has made me a better Gus.

That time in Vietnam was the most formative of my life.

Check on Amazon for my memoir *Welcome Home From Vietnam, Finally* and the historical medical mystery, *One Degree.*

To expand on the book's discussions please visit my YouTube videos:

Christmas Eve: https://youtu.be/KkEfCYalWDs?si=Ck82eZOO_FTZpuXV

Bob Nevins and Gus after 50 years: https://youtu.be/K1lDGREvFlA?si=2uA84H5iLlxrXLHx

The Agent Orange Travesty: https://youtu.be/o8Nn_ZQWkB8?si=AoSnl7XnKB0UDnlq

ECHOES enter interview: https://youtu.be/uftx794t9j0?si=8a-iB2eFAoGUVKEM

My Plea (Long version): https://youtu.be/FABdnrWKUiQ?si=LbqhZuK9Dj2Fyl2Y

Dust Off 326th Medical Battalion: https://youtu.be/eYQ_ImRSvbI?

Gus Kappler

si=GpGdoZJNfHrFq5Pe